First to Last

The Tale of a Biker

Dennis W. Lid

CCB Publishing
British Columbia, Canada

First to Last: The Tale of a Biker

Library and Archives Canada Cataloguing in Publication

Lid, Dennis W., 1937-
First to Last: The tale of a biker / written by Dennis W. Lid. – 1st ed.
ISBN 978-0-9781162-9-3
1. Lid, Dennis W., 1937-. 2. Lid, Dennis W., 1937- --Travel.
3. Motorcyclists--United States--Biography. 4. Soldiers--United
States--Biography. I. Title.
GV1060.2.L53A3 2007   629.227'5092   C2007-903660-0

All map diagrams contained herein by Daniel Lid.
Cover design by Digital Pulp Publishing.

Extreme care has been taken to ensure that all information presented in this book is accurate and up to date at the time of publishing. Neither the author nor the publisher can be held responsible for any errors or omissions. Additionally, neither is any liability assumed for damages resulting from the use of the information contained herein.

Publisher: CCB Publishing
             British Columbia, Canada
             www.ccbpublishing.com

Dedication

This book is dedicated to all aficionados of the two-wheeled conveyance known as...

the motorcycle.

Acknowledgments

I thank my wife, Bi Yu, for her constant support and encouragement during the composition of this book, and for her patience in listening to the numerous verbal renditions of each revised chapter thereof. I also thank Daniel Lid, my son, for the creation of the map graphics employed, and my daughter, Amy, who along with her brother rendered useful comments for manuscript refinement. My deep appreciation is extended to friend, Lou Ginex, and working associates, Daylanne Markwardt and Ridha Mikdadi, for their critical recommendations regarding edits and revisions to the final draft. Additionally, my sincerest thanks go to Toni Plummer, Will Standley, Genene Coté, Nicky Pittman and Paul Rabinovitch for their time, effort and guidance in the revision and publishing process. Finally, I wish to thank all my many motorcyclist friends and associates who shared the adventures and memories of all those great motorcycle rides through the decades of our lives. Peace brothers and sisters. And may we all arrive and meet again in motorcycle heaven.

Contents

FIRST TO LAST

Chapter One

The End

"For where thy treasure is, there also will thy heart be."
(MATT. VI. 21.)

We spend our lives searching for answers. There are many questions to be addressed in life, but the most important one that must be answered by each of us is, "Where does my treasure lie?" The answer to this question is of the utmost importance, since it results in the culmination of our search for the Holy Grail. Do you know where your treasure is?

This is the tale of a biker... a soldier... a man whose life's adventures are intertwined with the motorcycles he has owned and the experiences he has had. This saga will take you on a journey through the highlights, episodes and travails of that near-lifetime sojourn and the interesting events that occurred along the way. Perhaps when we have finished with this trek, you will be able to answer the key question in your own life – "Where is your treasure?" I think I know, at long last, where mine is.

It Happens to All of Us... The End of Riding Days

And so the journey begins – at the end. It happens to all of us sooner or later. Your time will come as well. It's the dreadful event or occasion that ends your riding days. For some, it's an accident or injury; for others an illness, and for still others it's old age or just plain loss of capability or interest that brings on the occasion. Whatever the reason, it happens, and your riding days are over. It's time to "hang up the spurs." For a true rider, a real biker, an aficionado of the two-wheeled conveyance called the motorcycle, that happening would seem to be an absolute tragedy… like the end of the world – except for the memories, that is. We have spent so much time collecting those memories throughout our lives, and carefully storing them in our brain-cell databanks, that we are not about to forget them. The memories sustain us after the actions and adventures have past. We recall them at will to lift our spirits and help us carry on with life, or existence, as the case may be.

Consider a fellow like Evel Knievel, who has reached the point of no return. He has been a daredevil to the extreme all his life, and successfully so. Yet multiple injuries, age, loss of flexibility and estimations of consequences have caused him to finally lose the edge. Now he tutors his son in the art and technique of extreme daredevil riding and exhibitionism. His son has become his alter ego. The master dreams his dreams and relinquishes the reins of control to the younger generation out of necessity. His time has come. His memories, indeed, are sufficient to endure what lies ahead on the remainder of his life's journey. Yet, I wonder where his treasure is now.

Sale of Last Bike

My time came in Japan about 12 years ago at the age of fifty-six. It was a fateful day in the fall of 1993 for yours truly, and all five-feet-eight inches of my brown-haired, blue-eyed, athletic, wiry and, otherwise, nondescript self. I remember standing on the sidewalk in front of the house watching a friend by the name of Jack Owen drive off on my last bike… as its new owner. Jack and I had been riding companions for many years in the Camp Zama Motorcycle Club of Sagamihara, Japan. It was a U.S. Army, Japan (USARJ) sponsored club located South of Tokyo – but more about that later. I was surprised that Jack bought my 1987 Kawasaki

Ninja 750 R, since he already owned a Yamaha 1150cc Virago. Perhaps he wanted to try a sport bike with the front-leaning driving position for a change, or maybe he just liked the looks and performance of it.

One year later, however, he sold the Ninja and kept his Virago. I guess he didn't like the front-leaning rest position after all. It takes some getting used to as compared to the upright sitting position of the Yamaha. The difference in posture equates to the difference between a sport bike and a cruiser. I never asked him why he sold it, and he never divulged his rationale. We parted company that day, and we had infrequent contact with one another for the next few years. The bike was the common denominator, you see, and when that link was severed, there was little basis for continuing our relationship. Work and other interests caused our paths to diverge and diluted our friendship. I eventually transferred to a new job and location back in the States and totally lost contact with my friend for several years.

As Jack drove the sleek, black, Kawasaki Ninja away from me and into the sunset that fateful day, he took a piece of my heart as well. He drove up the sidewalk and onto the road. I watched until he was out of sight, shading my eyes with my hand as bike and rider were silhouetted against the setting sun. Even after I could no longer hear the turbo-like drone, the heartbeat of the vertical four, I stood in place for a long time holding the check from the sale of my geisha, as I was fond of calling her. Now she was gone; there would be no replacement. The impact of that fact began to sink into my consciousness, as I stood there motionless. My eyes looked without seeing anything, like the "thousand-yard stare" of a warrior after the battle subsides. It dawned on me that the time had come to "hang up my spurs" and end my riding days.

It would take a while for me to really grasp the significance of that realization. After sharing the better part of my lifetime with the iron horse, what would I do without one? The weekends would seem to be a bit listless and empty; the camaraderie of riding companions non-existent. Good-bye to new motorcycle adventures, the adrenaline rush and the accumulation of fresh memories of the good times. Why then, must I stop riding now? The reasons that contributed to that conclusion will eventually surface during this journey of a biker's tale. Part of it has to do with the challenge, the search, the quest that I mentioned earlier, but there's more to it than that. All that's left now, and since that fateful day, is the memory of the motorcycles I once owned and the great times I had on all of them… from *First to Last*. Yet, the quest for the Holy Grail continues. Perhaps it's a relentless search until the very end – until one draws one's last breath.

Chapter Two

The Beginning

The prelude that ushered in my motorcycling days resided in the Thornhill Drive neighborhood where I grew up, my friends and our group activities. These elements, to one degree or another, were all instrumental in leading to my way of life as a motorcyclist.

Our neighborhood included a group of about 14 boys who were relatively the same age. My family moved into that neighborhood when I was seven years old. I became the best of friends with all the boys. We did practically everything together from forming our own Cub Scout Den to joining the same Boy Scout and Explorer Troops as we progressed through the years to high school age. We played all the usual games that kids play during our younger years, from football and baseball to kick-the-can and bicycle hikes. We built tree houses, made rafts, boats, and down-hill racing coasters, dug tunnels, ran cross-country bicycle courses complete with jumps, curves, water obstacles and mud traps, went on BB Gun hunts to kill lizards and snakes, and camped out under the stars on many a summer night. We were a tough and raucous bunch of daring rascals and pretty good at just about everything we tried to do. I guess you'd call us "hardcore," and therein lay one essential ingredient of a true motorcyclist.

Other essential aspects of a true motorcyclist began to emerge as well. All the things we did required planning, organization and action of one kind or another. A few of my friends and I were the leaders of the groups we formed for specific tasks during our games and activities. We did the planning and directing; then we and our groups followed through with action to complete the tasks. Leadership, and the formation of organizations and elements for a common purpose, would prove to be useful skills later in my life when it came to planning motorcycle trips and events, and organizing clubs, rides and activities. So then, leadership, organizational and planning abilities are still other essential aspects of a true motorcyclist. These talents and skills were developed during the prelude to my motorcycling days in the crucible of my youth. The neighborhood, my friends of bygone days and the activities we engaged in formed the foundation of and threshold to the world of motorcycling.

My life as a motorcyclist really began in earnest when I got a learner's permit for driving from the State of California at age 14. The permit allowed me to use a motorbike or moped to ride solo. Convincing my parents that I needed such a conveyance was critical but not difficult. My most persuasive argument was that I had a rather long newspaper route in the Montclair Hills between Oakland and Orinda. These rugged hills were part of the Coast Range Mountains running along the seacoast of Northern California. We lived on one of the many ridge fingers descending from the Skyline on a road called Thornhill Drive. The views were spectacular along the upper portions of Thornhill toward its juncture with Snake Road, which in turn, connected to Skyline Boulevard on the highest ridge of the Coast Range Mountains. One could see the entire San Francisco Bay area from these vantage points including the Golden Gate and Bay Bridges, Treasure and Alcatraz Islands, San Francisco, Oakland and the entire bay.

The newspaper route for the Post Enquirer was several miles long and went from the top of the ridge at Snake Road along Thornhill Drive to the bottom of the gulch near Mountain Boulevard. I needed dependable transportation to negotiate this route on a daily basis. My three-speed racing bike had been used for this task up until the time that I bought my first motorbike with proceeds from paper-route earnings, lawn cuttings and car washings. It was the paper route that gave me the edge in convincing my parents that the moped was a sound investment for business purposes. Of course, it provided for pleasure trips as well. The motorbike saved time and effort. It was a more efficient way of delivering newspapers and of making monthly monetary collections for the service. Albeit, it was probably a less frugal method of delivery because of gasoline, license, insurance and maintenance costs, but the time and effort saved were devoted to my school studies instead. Owning a bike also taught me driving responsibility, safety and how to take care of a vehicle.

I learned how to drive safely and responsibly in two ways: First, by taking a safe driving course for motorcyclists, and second, by on-the-road driving experience. The course actually came years after the actual driving experience for the simple reason that there were no formal motorcycle safety courses during my youth. These courses were established years later in response to the rising number of motorcycle accidents. I finally took such a course at Camp Zama, Japan during March of 1986 to renew my motorcycle license and reduce my insurance premium. The course concentrated on driving techniques such as counter-steering, emergency braking by evenly applying both front and rear brakes, maneuvering to avoid obstacles, recognition of international road signs and a myriad of other driving aspects. It focused primarily on defensive driving, proper signaling, appropriate motorcycling attire and safety factors.

It was the actual on-road driving experience that was my best teacher during the learning process. Giving myself enough room to stop when following the car in front of me, or avoiding tailgating, was one lesson. Another was the use of both defensive and offensive driving to avoid trouble. All your senses have to be alert when you ride. You must anticipate what other drivers will probably do and be prepared for the opposite reaction, too. I learned to use my engine brake first and then complete the halt with the front and rear wheel brakes. Equally important was the use of speed and maneuvering to get out of harm's way. Where to drive on the road was another critical factor so as not to be the victim of a carelessly opened car door, or of an oncoming driver's overstepping the centerline. Looking beyond the curve and keeping your line in negotiating it, then applying power at the apex to power out of the curve was a worthwhile lesson learned. Other valuable lessons were learning to slow down during periods of low visibility or wet weather, and keeping the bike as near vertical and as perpendicular as possible when driving across railroad tracks or painted surfaces on pavement, especially when wet. Using curb crawling and split-lane driving techniques, where legal, in a safe and sane manner so as not to startle and upset other drivers or encourage road rage were also beneficial lessons. Finally, and most importantly, I strove to be a true "knight of the road" in my motorcycle driving so as to give motorcycling and my own reputation a good name. Keep in mind that you are automatically enrolled in the brotherhood of the road from the time you buy your first motorcycle. Good road manners are part and parcel of that initial purchase. It's like keeping the faith.

The Influence of Tommy Llewellyn and Other Friends

The thought of my buying that motorbike in the first place was prompted by three of my friends: Lloyd Sorenson, Tommy Lewellin and Richard Jacobsen. Lloyd Sorenson was my buddy and neighbor from across the street. He was my age, blond haired and blue eyed, athletic and well liked by all the folks in our neighborhood. He was a leader-type personality, the Oakland Tribune Newspaper boy in our area, my major competition, and my best friend. Lloyd acquired a three-wheeled motor scooter for use on his paper route. That got me to thinking – good idea. The idea grew into the purchase of my first bike.

Tommy Lewellin was a friend from across the valley on the other ridgeline. Lloyd and Tommy were close friends from school; I was the third wheel in that relationship. Tommy and I were just casual friends, but he was the one who owned the motorbike that I eventually purchased. He was a couple of years older than I was, and he put the moped up for sale after buying a newer and more powerful motorcycle. He was hooked. Motorcycling was in his blood forever. Of course, I seized the opportunity presented and acquired his old motorbike. That started me along the same path that he seemed to be following.

Tommy had a catalytic effect on me. He was the guy who sold me the three-speed racing bicycle a couple of years earlier. I bought it cheap for twelve dollars. It needed new handgrips, a new pedal on one side, a gear-cable adjustment, a rear brake-cable and a paint job. I gave it all those things and had a first-class racing bike – the fastest, slickest bike in town. It was a beauty.

Tommy was a character with a heart of gold, an innovator and a daredevil. He always seemed to have a smile on his face and was a happy-go-lucky type of person. One day when he was showing us his new motorcycle, he rigged a sparkplug in the end of his muffler and exhaust pipe and hooked it up to a wire connected to the plug cap on the engine head. He cranked up the engine, and with each throb of the motor the exhaust pipe belched a two-foot flame of sparkplug- ignited exhaust gas. We were impressed, to say the least. It just shows you how nutty we were at that age, and what stupid chances we used to take. It also reveals the true character of the avid and dedicated future motorcyclist. We were innovators, daredevils, risk takers, and some were incurable romantics with hearts of gold.

Richard Jacobsen was the final influencing factor in my purchase of the motorbike. Richard lived on the opposing ridgeline, and he was one of my close friends from school. His amazing stories mesmerized me. Those piercing brown eyes accompanied by his intensity, facial contortions, hand gestures and slender body language, as he told his fascinating stories, are the attributes I remember most about Richard. What an imagination he had, and how well he could express it. His imaginings were contagious. He inflamed my mind and thoughts as well. Cowboys and Indians, BB gun hunts, bike hikes, camping trips, motor vehicle voyages, cops and robbers, and commandos – all were subjects of his wild stories. His epic renderings stirred my mind, heart and soul and prodded my spirit of adventure. That is how Richard influenced me.

I recall one episode in particular that illustrates Richard's rich imagination and its impact on me. We were horsing around on a BB gun hunt in the woods near an old deserted shack on stilts in the Montclair Hills. How it all started, I'm not quite sure, but we began shooting at one another and chasing each other through the woods, as though we were commandos on a raid pursuing the enemy. It was all in fun, of course, but we should have thought of the possible consequences. What if one of those BBs hit an eye? That could have caused blindness for life. I eventually ended up in the abandoned shack shooting out the window at Richard, who was in hot pursuit of me but still outside. He rushed the shack and ducked under it. I leaned out the open window and popped a shot at him from a distance of about 20 feet as he stuck his head out from under the shack. He tried to sneak a peek at me to determine my exact location before taking his shot. All of a sudden, he screamed in agony, dropped his BB gun and held his hands over his face as he fell to the ground. Fear struck me as I stood watching my friend writhing in pain. I immediately regretted having shot him, especially at such close range with only his head and upper body visible. It was too risky, and it was too late.

"You okay, Rich?" I queried.

He didn't answer. He just lay there breathing deeply. Suddenly and violently Richard lurched to the standing position grabbing his gun as he arose. He stepped out from the side of the house, turned and looked up at me with the fiercest squinty-eyed look I'd ever seen on his pain-grimaced face. He cocked his BB gun while staring at me with a look of rage and bolted toward the front door of the shack. I thought I'd had it. Richard was angry, and I was the target of his spleen. He charged through the front door, stopped and took up an aggressive stance. We both took aim at one another from a distance of 12 feet, held our fire, and then… I started laughing. His expression changed from one of anger to one of bewilderment.

"What's so funny?" he asked.

"You're okay, except for that 'strawberry' on your forehead, but you're okay otherwise. I thought I put your eye out with all the screaming you were doing, but all I did was give you one heck of a welt on the head. And that's proof that I won this game, isn't it?"

With a half-smirk and a half-smile he said: "Yea, I guess you got that right. Some game, uh? You know, I wasn't really mad, just wanted you to think so. Boy does my head hurt," and he lowered the gun as he held his head with his other hand. All was well except for the welt, which took some time to heal. Whew! What an episode. Worthy of note was that the winner of this dangerous but adventuresome game was the future motorcyclist. Uncanny, isn't it? Another characteristic of the dedicated motorcyclist is revealed. He's a person with an adventuresome nature and a sense of danger.

All in all, Lloyd was the confidant and competition; Tommy was the catalyst and provider; and Richard was the free spirit and spark that prompted me to take action. And so it started for me too, this business and love of motorcycling. It began with the acquisition of that first moped.

First Bike – A Rube Goldberg Learning Device

What kind of bike was it? My first motorbike was neither mass-produced nor a company-manufactured one. It was a homemade, individually designed and created conveyance. You might call it a Rube Goldberg, or a crudely improvised but innovative learning device. That first bike was nothing more than a glorified bicycle with an engine mounted above the rear wheel. The bicycle frame was reinforced, the suspension was improved with springs on the heavy gauge front forks, but the rear frame was rigid, as there was no swing arm or shock and spring. It had a small gas tank and a single-cylinder, air-cooled, four-stroke engine mounted above the small diameter motor scooter rear wheel and tire. Mounted on the front was a balloon-type tire on an ordinary bicycle wheel. It was chain driven, single geared and even had pedal-assist for getting started and negotiating steep hills. Its top speed was a rousing 35 mph. Finally, it was equipped with mechanical hand and foot brakes fore and aft. What a contraption it was. Yet, as a young teenager, I was greatly impressed by that first set of motorized wheels. The bike didn't just provide transportation but a means of mobility, freedom, independence and control. The style, power and adrenaline rush, however, would have to wait until years later. The novice moped was strictly a learning device, sufficient for scooting up and down the Northern California hills but not much more. Yet, it was a start, an initiation… a first bike.

An Introduction to a Biker's Way of Life

My first bike introduced me to the world of motorcycling. I became addicted to a sport and way of life that would last the better part of my lifetime. The motorcycle became a centerpiece of life, a common denominator so-to-speak. It provided a reason for starting conversations with perfect strangers, some of whom became fast friends. The bike was the subject of attention and served as the basis for both social and adventuresome experiences. Races, shows, rodeos, tournaments, expeditions and other events were oriented on the motorcycle. Even work depended on it.

At home the bike occupied my thoughts, time and effort as well. The maintenance and beautification of the beast, service and repairs, accessory items needed for bike and rider, and the money applied to all these items required my attention. Windscreen, helmet, goggles, gloves, boots, leathers, wet-weather gear, compass, toll-coin holder, tank or saddlebags, bungee cords, cover and cleaning paraphernalia were some of the critical items needed by an avid motorcyclist. All these things including insurance, license and registration came at a cost and over a period of time. Accessory items were not purchased all at once. Few riders could afford that. Yet, over the months and years, every biker could afford these accessories. The most essential items were selected for purchase first, followed by those less critical. Luxury items were acquired last if at all. Things like stereo sets with speakers and two-way radios were the ultimate indulgences and were seldom purchased. They were lowest on the rider's priority list.

A motorcyclist must be a dedicated individual to tolerate all the demands on time, effort and wallet. And, so, motorcycling became more than a sport in my life. It became a way of life. The simple moped, my first bike, introduced me to the biker's way of life. What a beautiful memory. You remember your first bike, too, don't you? It's as vivid in your mind as it was the day you bought it, isn't it? Some things we never forget. That's how it is with bikers and their mounts. First bikes are especially well remembered because after all, they are special in that they are "first."

My top priority after purchasing that motorbike, besides getting it registered, licensed and insured was to safely park it. Now that doesn't sound like much of a problem, does it? Normally it wouldn't be, but our house had a small, two-car garage. Our family car took up one parking space; our tenant's car occupied the second space. My moped had to fit somewhere in between the two cars and there was very limited room. The handlebars of the moped had to be raised above the level of both cars' fenders so as not to scratch them. The solution was the construction of a wooden ramp for the front wheel only, so as to lift the handlebars higher than the car fenders when the motorbike was parked. The trick was to make sure that I parked the bike before both cars arrived in their parking spaces each evening. Timing was critical. If I misgauged it, or came home late, then my dad would have to back his car out of the garage to permit access of my bike to its ramped parking area without scratching either car. Needless to say, I was reluctant to impose on my father's kind nature any more than was absolutely necessary. This exercise, however, was required on several occasions and taught me an important lesson: "For every action there is an equal and opposite reaction." Having to interrupt my father made me think things through before I acted and to be aware of the possible consequences. It was a good lesson for life. I wish I had kept it in mind more often as I pursued my own.

The years passed; we boys grew up. By the time we graduated from our respective high schools, each of us followed different paths in pursuing our lives. Contact between us was eventually lost as our individual courses diverged over time. People moved, some took civilian jobs and others went on to college or into the military. Our first motorbikes and scooters were sold; old friendships faded. We struck out along life's road into an unknown adult future. Our quest finally began in earnest. Such was the prelude to our motorcycling lives.

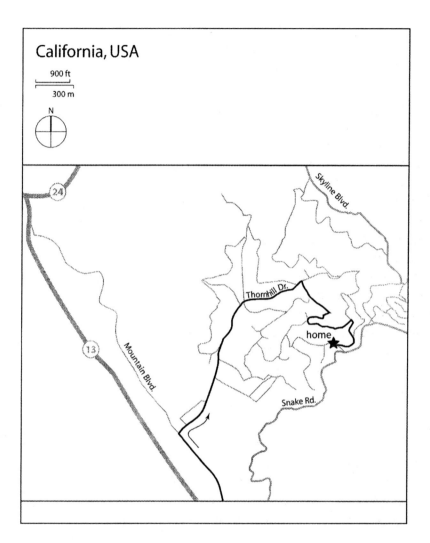

California Map (Thornhill Drive)

Chapter Three

Interruption

Years of Drought Without a Bike

It was the dry period – a time without a motorcycle that lasted seven years. My life as a biker had just begun during my teenage years and a long interruption had already intervened. This drought was like a plague or blight on my life. There would be other periods like it in the future. They would be memorable only by their extreme monotony. "Into every life a little rain must fall." Yet, the quest continued even during the dry years.

My fledgling biker's life was severely interrupted when the family moved and I was sent off to boarding school. I had to sell the motorbike. There was no choice in the matter; it simply had to be done. My parents took a chance, garnered all the cash they could muster from their known assets, threw in with a partner and went into the resort and hotel business. When the house was sold and their first resort lodge at Lake Tahoe was purchased, I became a bike-less boarding student at Saint Mary's High School located in Peralta Park, California. What a change it was compared to the nice home we had on Thornhill Drive in Montclair. The school was fine, but housing for boarding students, though appreciated, was very old and decrepit. It remained rather inhospitable even after a homemade paint job of my two-man room. Peter Hookendyjke, my Dutch roommate, and I made the best of it. We dwelt and studied there for the next two years until graduation from high school gave us relief. Both of us then went off to the University of Santa Clara in California, Peter as a Mechanical Engineering student and myself into Liberal Arts as an English Major. I graduated four years later; Peter left for Holland after completing his junior year. He didn't graduate. I never heard from him again and didn't know the reason for his abrupt departure. Word had it that there was a family problem of some sort, and that he joined the Dutch Air Force after returning home. Some friendships end abruptly and are never reestablished, as was the case with this one. God speed was my wish for him.

Finishing School and Beginning Work

I chose the University of Santa Clara because it was close, affordable and my application was accepted there. The business my parents engaged in at Lake Tahoe didn't last. The partners didn't get along well and so dissolved their business affiliation. Each traded their share of the partnership for a smaller commercial property and went their separate way. My folks ended up in Menlo Park owning and managing a restaurant and quaint hotel by the name of the Marie Antoinette Inn. It was close enough to Santa Clara for me to live at home, even though I preferred boarding at the university. I lived and worked at home during my freshman year, and then I bought an old 1948 Chevrolet convertible and became a boarding student at the university. It was more convenient and conducive to studying, and my father was willing to pay the boarding costs. Those college days constituted four long, hard and boring years with the exception of my writing, drama and military ROTC classes. I knew I needed a degree, but I didn't really know what I wanted to do. Perhaps I'd end up in teaching, or the military or who knows what. Anyway, the bachelor's degree was an essential first step; it was a necessary ticket-punch for the professional life. That sheepskin was a mandatory requirement for a successful life in the 1950's era. So I endured unto graduation and received my degree and lieutenant's commission into the regular army.

After graduation, the United States Army took over my life. Wow! What a change. Since I wanted more than "three hots and a cot" to start off my military career, the first thing I did was to partner up and get married so as to start my family life just prior to entering the service. I won't dwell on that mistake, since it ended in failure eleven years and two children later. Let's just say I shamefully added to the divorce statistic and disrupted a few lives. I'm not proud of it, but it's a fact, and I contributed to the mess. A decade later, after a bit of alimony and years of child support payments, the marriage was annulled. It was a very negative and disillusioning time of life for all concerned. The quest for the Holy Grail seemed all but halted. Even thoughts of motorcycles and the life of a biker were temporarily shelved. I was like a blind man groping in the dark for quite some time. I began to see the light at the end of the tunnel a number of years later and started living life again. The bottom line to this part of my life is that divorce or annulment is an episode to be avoided if at all possible. The best way to ensure that is to be wise enough to choose the right spouse to begin with. As Shakespeare once wrote, "All this the world well knows, yet few know well how to shun the heaven that leads men to this hell." Let's leave it at that.

Acclimatization to Army Life

After attending Infantry Officer's Basic Course and Airborne training, I was assigned to Fort Lewis, Washington for three years of Infantry duty with the 2d Battle Group, 47th Infantry. For another year, I attended the Defense Language Institute at Monterey, California, and studied the Vietnamese Language and culture. Thereafter, I went off to war in Southeast Asia as a Military Assistance and Advisory Group (MAAG) Army Battalion Advisor. That lasted for half-a-year in the Central Highlands of Vietnam in II Corps at a place called Tan Canh near Dak To. Things experienced on combat operations in the highlands will fill another book some day. I finished my combat tour of duty at Tuy Hoa on the coast of the South China Sea as a Psychological Operations Officer advising the South Vietnamese Army G5 Section (Psychological Operations) at that location. That was "fun time" as well, but the telling of those experiences is reserved for a more appropriate time and place. The basic lesson learned was that war is an ugly and numbing experience best avoided if at all possible. It should definitely be a last choice in attempts to rectify the human condition. Yet, in a humble and belated defense of the Vietnam War, and in the words of a respected source, I dare to say:

> *War is an ugly thing, but not the ugliest of things; the decayed and degraded state of moral and patriotic feeling which thinks that nothing is worth war is much worse. A man who has nothing for which he is willing to fight; nothing he cares about more than his own personal safety; is a miserable creature who has no chance of being free, unless made and kept so by the exertions of better men than himself.*
> *(John Stuart Mill, 1806-1873)*

Each of us searches in our own way for our treasure, though there seem to be many obstacles and detours along the path toward the Holy Grail. Our earnest hope is that we will arrive one day.

During all the years from high school through college and the first several years of army service, my only contact with the biker's world was through reading motorcycle magazines, attending a few races and engaging in conversations with motorcycle enthusiasts and bike owners. Most of my time was devoted to other concerns from studies to girls, guns to cars, and marriage and family to army duties.

After becoming an army careerist, I took up an interest in handguns to fill the void left by the absence of motorcycles in my life. It helped ease the pain of not having a bike. I bought a 38-caliber over/under Derringer pistol. It was chrome plated with hardwood handgrips. The pistol looked great, but its accuracy at more than ten feet left much to be desired. Yet, the weapon served its purpose. It was simple and effective for close-range personal protection; easy to load, aim and fire; and practically maintenance free. Over the years there were additions to the handgun arsenal in the form of a 45-caliber Colt automatic and a 9-millimeter Smith & Wesson automatic. However, these handguns didn't exactly provide an adrenalin rush, as did a motorcycle. That nagging urge to get a bike kept haunting me, but I had to be practical. A car was the first priority.

That first car, a '48 Chevy convertible, took the place of my motorbike through the college years. I fixed it up to "cherry" condition like it was straight from the factory. A Chevrolet dealer in San Francisco made an offer for the car after its restoration was completed, but I turned him down. First cars and first bikes are the same – very special. I bought that Chevy instead of purchasing a new motorcycle, as it seemed to be more logical to get a car at the time. I had to haul baggage, books, lab supplies, family, friends and other cargo under all weather conditions during those years. This proved to be the case in the future with all the other cars I owned as well. My heart wanted the bike, but my head told me to buy the car. And so I did. It was the right thing to do under the circumstances, and I don't regret taking that action. It's just that the bike was always in the back of my mind as the thing I wanted to own. The car was simply a more practical choice, and it remained so for all the years to come. The lesson for all bike enthusiasts is that a man must establish priorities. A car is a higher priority item than a motorcycle to a family man. And, so, a biker must learn to bide his time and save his shekels toward the day when he can afford both car and motorcycle. That takes time, sacrifice, dedication and frugality, but the dream can be realized. A true motorcyclist ensures that it is realized sooner or later. Patience! All good things come to those who wait… patiently.

Speaking of patience, the day finally arrived when my first Vietnam tour of duty came to an end and I returned to the United States as a Captain. The army assigned me to Fort Benning, Georgia as a "snowbird" working in the G1, Personnel Staff Office. A "snowbird" is a temporarily assigned person who is waiting for a school, course, or other time-critical assignment to begin. My Infantry Officer's Advanced Course was due to start in about four months. It would be a nine month course of instruction in preparation for future command and staff duties. In the meantime, I worked in the G1 Office (Personnel) on miscellaneous staff functions. It was pretty dull. Then, suddenly, the light dawned. I was making pretty good pay as a Captain, had a new Chevy station wagon with easy monthly payments, the family lived in economical on-post housing, and there was discretionary income left over after paying the monthly bills. Guess what? The interruption was over. It was time to buy another motorcycle and resume my life as a biker. And so the search continued.

Vietnam Map

Chapter Four

Resurrection And Resumption

Back to Motorcycling

The resurrection and resumption of my life as a motorcyclist occurred during the assignment to Fort Benning, Georgia, after my return from Vietnam. I picked up where I had left off seven years earlier when I sold my first motorbike, and it was back to motorcycling with a vengeance. I purchased my second bike; it was a Ducati 125cc (125 cubic centimeter engine) street version. The bike was a decent utility model for reentering the biker's world. Granted, it was nothing fancy as far as looks and performance were concerned. The 125cc street version was not known for speed or power. The bike was renowned for dependability, economy and general-purpose around-town riding. It got me to work and back and provided modest weekend enjoyment, mostly as a means to visit the motorcycle shop and talk with its owners and mechanics.

The Bike Shop

I spent many Saturdays visiting the Ducati motorcycle shop on the main drag leading to the front gate of Fort Benning. Cecil and his wife, the owners of the shop, Jack, their mechanic, and I became fast friends. They had me pegged right as a future customer for the sale of one of their new Ducatis and for necessary bike services thereafter. Besides that, they were decent, honest folks and good neighbors with a genuine sense of southern hospitality. They were "salt of the earth" type people. We talked about bikes and motorcycle events, puttered around the shop, shared stories with riders who stopped to look at the new models and tinkered with repairs being made on some of the used bikes. The owners told me all about the Ducati brand of motorcycles, and the mechanic showed me their inner workings as he went about repairing engines, transmissions, brakes, suspensions, electronics, exhausts, and other vital parts and accessories. I learned a lot from them during my Ducati years. On future bike excursions, I would make use of that knowledge to effect repairs and adjustments on my own iron horses. Our conversations also increased my interest in all aspects of motorcycling from shop ownership, management and sales, to service, repairs and accessories. I gained an appreciation for everything that was involved in the motorcycle business and for the people who participated in that endeavor. All this information and interest enhanced my life as a motorcyclist and whetted my appetite for the purchase of that second bike. The time was finally at hand, the money was in the bank and I was ready to ride. The resurrection of my life as a motorcyclist had finally arrived.

"Do you want the black and red bike or the black and blue one?" Cecil asked.

"I want the black and red, 125cc Ducati – that 'plain Jane' model up front," I replied.

Cecil and his wife just smiled. They knew how much I wanted a motorcycle. They just wanted to make sure it was the right one.

"You're sure you don't want the larger 250cc model?" queried Cecil's wife.

I looked over at the bigger bike, felt somewhat intimidated by its size and answered:

"No thanks, the 125cc will do for now," and I wondered how long the "now" would last.

Cecil and his wife exchanged a quick glance with one another. They knew something I didn't know. It was the fact that beginners usually don't anticipate their own needs very well. From past experience, they knew that I would be seeking a bigger displacement bike in short order. That's what they were trying to tell me, but I wasn't listening. I was convinced that I should resume my life as a motorcyclist with a more modest bike for starters. After all, this was a resurrection after seven years of no riding. I would find out the hard way, down the road, that I should have purchased the larger displacement bike after all. Yes, I should have been bolder in the choice of which bike to buy. Rather than just putting my toe in the water, so to speak, I should have aggressively jumped in the deep end of the pool. I should have purchased the larger displacement motorcycle for my resurgence into the biker's world. It would have saved time and been cheaper in the long run. The bike shop owners were only trying to satisfy the customer and keep from offending a friend when they conceded to selling me the smaller motorcycle. We exchanged the money for the bike, and I was once again a motorcyclist. Resurrection!

The Ducati Years

Getting back to riding again was a great experience in itself. The sense of freedom, independence and control, and the joy of being immersed in the environment, at one with my surroundings and in tune with nature were extremely gratifying. The physical sensations of warmth from the sun, wind in the face and hair, vibrations from the engine through frame, seat and handlebars, and sounds from the deep-throated exhaust contributed to feelings of harmony, satisfaction and well-being. Everything just felt right. Life was good and seemed complete again. Funny what a motorcycle can do for a fellow, especially when like-minded people are involved.

31

The bike shop mechanic and I teamed up as riding buddies and rode with a nearby motorcycle club. This was my first exposure to group motorcycle rides. It was instructive and interesting. Riding with a group of bikers required discipline and consideration of others. The safety and hegemony of the group took precedence over individual preferences. Learning the visual signals, both hand and light, and passing these on to the long line of riders was essential. Staggered formation driving, forming dual columns or single file configurations, avoiding road and traffic hazards, and watching out for fellow bikers were also primary requirements for club riding. Predictable, smooth and harmonious driving were most desirable traits. The group rides taught me these things as the club made its way through parts of Georgia and Alabama on several excursions through the year. I also determined on these trips that the 125cc Ducati was a bit underpowered. Thoughts of a bigger displacement bike began to form in my mind. One of our rides took us to the drag strip in Alabama across the Chattahoochee River from Columbus, Georgia. It was at that time that the shop mechanic and I first considered getting involved in drag racing motorcycles (quarter mile speed sprints from a dead stop). In the months that followed, we pursued the idea with zeal and made it a reality.

The need for speed and excitement is almost overwhelming in a young person. Noticeably lacking during the early Ducati stage of my life was the adrenaline rush. I tried free-fall parachuting with the army club at Fort Benning to help satisfy the urge. That helped, but it wasn't enough. Nor was the little Ducati. I had been eyeing a bigger, more powerful "crotch rocket" at the bike shop. It was a bright red Ducati 250cc, single-pot thumper, air-cooled, four-stroke, Mark III road racer. I realized the vision I had on the club rides of a larger displacement motorcycle, and I traded the 125cc for the Mark III. I couldn't help myself; I had to have it. It was my ticket to the adrenaline rush via road racing and drag racing. My mechanic was ecstatic as well. He got to test drive the road racer after tuning and race prepping it.

The Mark III was as sleek as a bullet in the wind and looked like it was going 100 mph when it was standing still. With its straight-through, tuned megaphone attached in place of the street-legal muffler and exhaust pipe, it wasn't exactly quiet. This fact did not much endear me to the local population. You've got to keep the "revs" up to produce the power for the speed, and when you do… what a rush! The Mark III incorporated only the essentials and was austere in appearance, fast and versatile in performance, and a bit temperamental. It was not only a speedy road racer for its day but made a respectable showing at the drag strip as well.

The Drag Strip

The bike, my mechanic and I took on all comers in our class at the drag strip in Alabama across the river from Columbus, Georgia, and beat most of them. I remember one fellow in particular driving a 250cc Honda Hawk. He tried everything he could think of to increase the speed of his bike off the line, including the removal of the tuned exhaust pipes, which only eliminated the back-pressure on the twin heads and reduced the performance of his bike. He was one frustrated puppy as he suffered his losses.

The Ducati reigned supreme at the drag strip. The trick to winning was a good start and staying on the top of the RPM curve down the strip. Clutch and throttle work were critical. Keeping the front end of the bike down with the front tire contacting the pavement as I slipped the clutch and turned on the throttle were the keys to success for a good take-off from the line. This had to be timed exactly, accomplished quickly and executed expertly so as to maintain a fast but straight line down the drag strip. Any mistake would ruin the start and cost the race.

The second phase of the motorcycle drag race, once off to a good start, required peaking out the "revs" through the gear train, and staying on top of the RPM curve. This process squeezed the maximum power and speed from each gear. Once again, speed and timing in working through the gears were the essential factors for victory at the drag strip. As they say, "Practice! Practice! Practice!" And a well-tuned bike brought about a winning combination. A good mechanic, a fast bike and an expert driver were the ingredients that spelled success at drag racing. Such were the Ducati years – but the quest continued.

1. "I remember standing on the sidewalk in front of the house watching a friend drive off on my last bike… as its new owner" (Zama, Japan)

2. "All that's left is the memory of the motorcycles I once owned… " (My last bike: a 1987 Kawasaki Ninja 750 R)

3. "My first bike was a glorified bicycle with an engine mounted above the rear wheel." (A Rube Goldberg invention, circa 1953)

4. "The Mark III (Ducati) was fast and versatile, though a bit temperamental." (Road racing and drag stripping in Alabama)

5. "A 1968 Kawasaki 175cc dirt bike became my new bike."
(Kadina and Naha, Okinawa scrambles tracks)

6. Scrambles race starting lineup at Kadina, Okinawa in 1968

7. Kadina, Okinawa scrambles track race with my number 111
Kawasaki 175cc in the lead. (Kadina, Okinawa circa 1968)

8. "Number 111 still in the lead at Kadina, Okinawa scrambles."
(Kadina Okinawa circa 1968)

9. Over the jump and into the final turn at Kadina scrambles race in 1968 on the way to a trophy. (Okinawa, 1968)

10. The Bultaco 200cc that took first place by half-a-wheel length over my Kawasaki 175cc. (Kadina, Okinawa scrambles races 1968)

11. My *Hakka* gal and I on the road – "How sweet it is."
(At Nikko, Japan, and remembering Grass Mountain, Taiwan)

12. Capt. Fred Jones (left), his bike and Lieut. George McAuliffe at
RECONDO. (Training area, Koolau Mountains, Oahu, Hawaii 1977)

13. Solo on my first touring and cruising bike… a Honda CX-500cc rabbit-ear twin. (Camp Zama, Japan 1983)

14. The CX-500 Honda provided comfort for two-up riding on low-speed touring. (Camp Zama, Japan 1983)

15. Ready to roll, family style, on my CX-500 Honda mini-cruiser. (Camp Zama, Japan 1984)

16. "I enjoyed the camaraderie and pleasure of touring all over Japan with the Zama Motorcycle Club. (Nikko, Japan)

Chapter Five

The Missouri Connection

The United States Army is a fair, understanding and well-disciplined organization which demands much from its personnel, and which treats them with mutual respect and dignity. A soldier must keep in mind, however, that the needs of the army always come first. "Duty, Honor and Country" are not just a slogan to a military man. They are gospel; they are sacrosanct.

I completed the Infantry Officer's Advanced Course at Fort Benning. Thereafter, I received reassignment orders and proceeded to Fort Leonard Wood, Missouri with family, bag and baggage, but minus the Ducati. I sold the Mark III, thinking that I wouldn't have much time to ride because I was assuming a command position at Leonard Wood.

The two primary career-track assignments that every military careerist strives for are command and staff. Command assignments at company, battalion, brigade and higher echelon are rare. There simply aren't enough of these positions in the army to give all officers a crack at being a commander. Yet, a successfully executed command position is a necessary "ticket-punch" for promotion to higher grade and for increased responsibility and authority within the military. This is especially true of the combat arms such as the Infantry, the Queen of Battle. Conversely, an unsuccessfully executed command assignment is usually a career stopper. Career development through successful accomplishment of the company commander post was my top priority. This was my rationale for selling the Ducati, Mark III prior to leaving Fort Benning. I thought that the concentration on my new assignment would preclude having any time to ride.

My rationale was flawed; I was mistaken. After getting settled at Leonard Wood in on-post housing and becoming entrenched in the job, I discovered that life was slow and rather monotonous during my off time. It turned out that there was ample opportunity to ride on some weekends despite the demands of work at the company. I felt the need for another motorcycle and began my search for a used bike.

Fort Leonard Wood is two hours away from Saint Louis, Missouri by car. The fort was definitely out in the woods and had limited entertainment possibilities. This was so much the case that I began to have doubts about continuing my military career. Marital difficulties added to the problem during this period. Things were so dull and disheartening during off-duty time that I actually applied for employment with the Central Intelligence Agency (CIA). I simultaneously processed my conditional resignation papers from the army. The conditions were that I be offered an assignment to language school, training in Special Forces (Green Berets) and reassignment to Southeast Asia. If the army agreed to these three conditions, I would agree to remain on active duty rather than resign.

I went through the entire application process with the CIA including the interviews at Langley, Virginia during a short leave. The agency accepted me, subject to my being honorably discharged from the army. Their offer was for a career position with the CIA. The Vietnam War was a hot issue at the time. My infantry, airborne, Vietnamese language and combat experience were assets eagerly sought by the agency. They wouldn't have to spend too much time or money training me for the position of a Field Operations Officer in Vietnam. To the best of my knowledge, the CIA applied moderate pressure on the Pentagon to give favorable consideration to approving my request for resignation from the army.

After my trip to Langley, I proceeded to the Pentagon to discuss my resignation request. To my total surprise and great relief, the army agreed to my requested conditions for remaining on active duty in the regular army, provided that I withdraw my resignation request immediately. I did so. After returning to Leonard Wood, I notified the CIA that I had decided to remain in the army and turned down the agency's kind offer of employment. I remained in my company command assignment at Leonard Wood for another year thereafter. My cadre trained one large company after another, back to back, throughout the year, and then sent the men off to Advanced Infantry Training (AIT) and ultimately to Vietnam. One year later, I received orders from the Department of the Army to proceed to the State Department Language School in Alexandria, Virginia to attend a nine-month Lao Language course. Thereafter, I was to proceed to Fort Bragg, North Carolina for Special Forces training and then on to Okinawa for assignment with the 1st Special Forces Group Airborne or 1st SFGA. This unit was providing Special Forces teams for missions to Southeast Asia at that time. The army was true to their word and kept their end of the bargain, as did I. "Now," I thought, "what about getting another bike for a little stress relief?"

Initiation to Off-road Riding

I found another bike at the local motorcycle shop. It was outside the main gate of Fort Leonard Wood and up the road at the intersection with the highway bound for Saint Louis. This was a Honda shop. The owner specialized in converting street bikes into dirt bikes for trail and enduro riding. He was working on a new 90cc Honda "putt putt" when I met him for the first time. He had taken off the fenders and battery covers, put on knobby tires and skid plate, and then changed the gearing to accommodate off-road riding. He was working on the suspension system when I asked:

"Isn't that an awfully small bike for trail riding?"

"Nope," he answered.

I'd find out more about that 90cc Honda later, much to my chagrin. It was a lot more bike than it appeared to be. That was the reason for his trite reply. He knew whereof he spoke.

"Can I help you with something?" he queried.

"Sure! Sell me that silver and black Honda 161cc street bike out front."

"Okay," he replied, "let's talk turkey."

And so we did. I purchased the used Honda 161cc, four-stroke, vertical twin for a reasonable price and was back in business with the motorcycle world. Subsequent visits to the shop would solicit invitations from the owner to trail rides and enduro races.

Off-road riding was in vogue at Fort Leonard Wood, Missouri during the 1960's. So my first priority was to convert the newly acquired street bike to an off-road dirt bike. I mimicked the shop owner's modifications to his 90cc Honda and applied those innovations to my 161cc Honda. Off came the unnecessary covers and casings, fenders and muffler; on went the lower gearing, stiffer suspension, skid-plate and knobby tires. He must have modified his engine with a bore and valve job, although he never acknowledged that this was the case, whereas my engine remained stock. The result was that his bike, though smaller, was a fast, lean machine at the lower end of the speed spectrum; mine was a quick, heavy machine at the mid-range of the speed spectrum. The 90cc Honda was fast off the line and highly maneuverable but began to level off in performance at a speed of about 30 mph. The 161cc Honda was slower off the line due to its additional weight and slightly less maneuverable because of its larger frame, but much better in performance at speeds in excess of 25 mph as a result of its larger displacement engine. I decided that the modifications to my Honda were adequate for trail and enduro riding. Now it was test time.

Trail Riding on Earth and Ice

I did trail riding and enduro racing for the next year. The first test was against several bikes, including the 90cc Honda, on a trail ride. I'll never forget that first night trail ride that the bike shop owner talked me into joining with a few of his biker friends. It was my initiation into off-road endeavors, and as the "newbie," I was a sitting duck. It was a setup. They were familiar with the terrain, trails and off-road riding, but I was not. I learned the hard way that night. I had modified the Honda by reducing as much weight as possible, but had to add a skid-plate and leave the lights in place. Whatever else could be removed from the bike to reduce weight was eliminated. In those days (1965), we had to make our own dirt bikes by converting street bikes. At any rate, the trail ride began with a swift entry into the woods. It was all I could do to keep the taillight of the bike in front of mine in view. Then, all of a sudden, that taillight went out, or I thought it did. Actually, the biker in front of me had turned a hard left, following the trail up the ridge. I missed the sharp left turn in the trail and flew off a steep twenty-five foot incline, arse over tea kettle, and ended up on my back at the bottom of the gulch with the bike next to me; handlebars askew with bent brake and clutch levers and a broken taillight lens. Other than that, horse and rider sustained no major damage. Then I heard the bikers on the trail above having a good laugh, and I knew I'd been had. They helped me get the Honda out of the gully and back in running shape up on the trail. From that time on, I was a member of their club.

The next test came during the winter after the first light snowfall. Normally one does not ride motorcycles on ice and snow, but don't tell that to the motorcyclists in Missouri. They have a favorite sport during the late fall and early winter. It's called ice cycling or racing on the ice. We didn't go so far as to use-spiked tires and actually race one another on an ice track or frozen lake, but we did compete on snow-trail riding and ice-creek skidding in the Rolla, Missouri woods. Snow and ice riding is a unique and bizarre experience. It is easy to lose the snow-covered trail and almost impossible to control a bike's direction and speed on an icy surface. Forget about braking altogether on ice. It just doesn't work. Slow, smooth and deliberately delicate execution of all maneuvers, acceleration and engine braking are essential driving techniques in this environment. Agile footwork in response to the bike's fishtailing, slipping and sliding is another requirement for this type of riding. The value of a lightweight, small displacement bike proves its worth in ice and snow riding. The smaller motorcycles can literally run circles around the larger bikes on ice and snow. Amateurs beware! Even the professionals find this kind of riding challenging. Snow and ice cycling are strictly for off-road riding. The strange sensations associated with the challenge of maintaining some degree of control over speed and direction are what make this riding so exciting. Only experienced riders should attempt it – and with an abiding respect at that.

Enduro Racing

Those same experienced riders taught me the ropes of endurance racing as winter ended and spring ensued. Enduro racing requires stamina, strength and endurance on the part of the rider and a good dirt bike with high ground clearance and long-travel suspension as well. As a converted street bike, my 161cc Honda proved not to be a very good enduro dirt bike. It had three fatal flaws that prevented it from being a good off-road performer. It was heavy, had low ground clearance and soft, short-travel suspension. I put the bike through its paces on enduro races but failed to rapidly and efficiently negotiate mud bogs, stream banks and vertical log and wall obstacles. Running those races completely exhausted me. They were fun but grueling. I never won an enduro race, but I sure wore myself out trying to do so with those great riders of the Missouri connection. The year passed quickly with the job, running the trails and enduro racing, and then it was time to be reassigned.

Alexandria, Virginia became my family's home for the next year. I rigged the Honda for street riding by replacing the tires, removing the skid plate, softening the suspension, re-gearing and re-sprocketing it. After putting the fenders, covers and muffler on, it provided decent transportation to the job and back. Work consisted of Lao Language School after a three-month stint of "snow birding" at Fort Meyer, Virginia until the school started. I enjoyed solo weekend road riding and visits to local historical sites during this period. The year passed. I graduated, sold the Honda and went on leave en route to my new duty station. And life's journey went on.

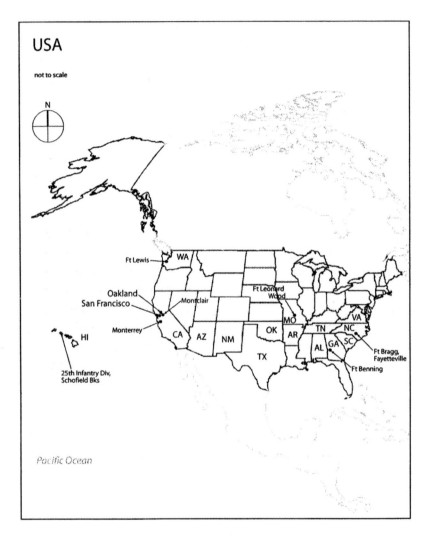

USA Map

Chapter Six

Interlude

Leave and Restlessness

On leave for a few weeks in California without a bike is a worst-case scenario. Leave is for rest and relaxation. Without my stress-relief valve, a motorcycle, rest and relaxation were difficult to accomplish. The family settled contentedly into new quarters on the civilian economy in Mountain View. This was in fairly close proximity to the in-laws' place located in Los Gatos. I spent two weeks working at their ranch assisting in the construction of a new stable for their horses. Although the family seemed satisfied, being on leave and working at the ranch made me nervous and restless. Piddling around on leave just aggravated the situation, especially since the in-laws and I didn't get along that famously. I was anxious to get on with my career, attend the Special Forces Course and proceed to Okinawa to join the 1st Special Forces Group Airborne. Everything else seemed incidental and irrelevant.

My family didn't understand my anxiety and neither did I until much later. This anxious restlessness, like a volcano ready to explode within me, was symptomatic of and foreshadowed a marital estrangement. Why else would a man volunteer and look forward to going off to war for a second time? A person wants to remain with loved ones when the heart is content. Was this volunteerism simply another way of seeking an adrenalin rush, of acquiring career-progression kudos or was it, perhaps, a kind of obscure death wish?

New Honda Scrambler

The need for excitement, adventure and challenge are part of everyone's nature. In some people, these needs are more acute than in others. Type "A" personalities require a heavy dose of these elements for a sense of fulfillment. My sense of fulfillment was "chafing at the bit" during my leave. The temporary solution, as always, was a motorcycle experience. In this case, it took the form of a motorcycle expedition. The family agreed that purchasing a bike for the trip to Fort Bragg, North Carolina and for use thereat was a good solution to the transportation problem. The car would remain with the family in California; the bike would go to Bragg. I would have to start immediately since the trip would take about one week. However, first things first, I had to buy a bike.

My last motorcycling experience in Missouri was with off-road riding. I must have had that phenomenon subconsciously in mind while shopping for a bike for the trip to Bragg. Straight thinking would dictate the purchase of a cruiser or touring bike for a long highway journey and daily use at Fort Bragg thereafter. Yet, the Missouri connection and its influence directed my efforts toward the selection of a scrambler, an off-road motorcycle. Now that's the worst possible choice for a lengthy, high-speed cross-country excursion. My being a contrarian helped seal the bargain. I bought a new Honda 305cc Scrambler. It was red and gray with a hefty frame and had long travel suspension. This was Honda's first attempt at building a manufactured, out-of-the-box scrambler. It was a reasonably good attempt for a first-time effort, but it was too bulky and heavy by today's scrambler standards. The bike did have eye-appeal and sufficient power in its four-stroke engine to make the trip, and it somehow appealed to my fancy at the time. I paid cash, and it was mine.

The next few days were spent in preparation for the trip. I purchased a few essential items such as wet-weather gear, helmet, gloves, rucksack and bungee cords. My boxed up uniforms and training gear were sent to Fort Bragg. I bid adieu to the family and drove the scrambler for five days from Los Gatos, California to Fort Bragg, North Carolina.

The Trip from San Jose, CA to Fort Bragg, NC

It was an interesting trip that started in the warmth of the California sun and ended in the chill of the North Carolina rain. I headed south from San Jose on Route 101 to Paso Robles, east on Highway 46 to Bakersfield and Interstate 40 for the rest of the trip to North Carolina. It was a pleasant ride through California's hills, valleys and the Mojave Desert. I arrived at Flagstaff, Arizona and remained overnight (RON) on that first night after a long day on the bike. I was bone weary and stayed at a comfortable hotel. The next day, I headed east on the interstate toward Albuquerque, New Mexico and on to Amarillo, Texas before stopping for the night. During a sand storm on the high plateaus of New Mexico, the scrambler lost power and sounded like it was not firing properly. I stopped and cleaned the air cleaner, gapped the sparkplug, fiddled with the carburetor and reset the points. It still didn't run right. I kept going, cleared the storm and dropped down in elevation as I entered Texas. The bike ran smoothly again after that. The lower elevation cured the problem of the air and gas mixture in the carburetor permitting the bike to run smoothly once again. I took the bike to a Honda shop in Amarillo for service before continuing the journey. That used up some precious time along the way, but it was a necessary delay. Preventive maintenance was the best guarantee of a carefree trip. The scrambler was holding up very well, which is more than I can say for the driver.

The long hours in the saddle were beginning to take their toll by day three. The drive from Amarillo, Texas to Fort Smith, Arkansas was uneventful except for the bugs and the dizzying experience of seeming to be going downhill all the way through Oklahoma. I attribute that false perception to having spent too much time on the road during the hours of darkness, and partly in the rain. The service stop for the bike caused a late departure, and so I had to drive across the Texas Panhandle and Oklahoma predominantly at night. The wear and tear on the driver was beginning to show as I arrived at Fort Smith for the third night's stay.

The next day was murky and overcast. Rain and cold were in store for this rider on day four of the journey. I suited up in my wet-weather gear and confronted the elements all the way through Arkansas and Tennessee from Fort Smith to a place called Rockwood, Tennessee for the fourth night's RON. The countryside was beautiful through the Great Smoky Mountains, even in the bad weather. Admittedly, though, the wet and cold got to me by the end of that long day. You know you are tired to the extreme when you do stupid things like coming to a complete stop at the top of the mountain pass of the Great Smoky Mountains to wait out a deluge of rain. All the cars and trucks stopped because the rain was so heavy that they couldn't see well enough to safely continue. I did the same, momentarily, until realizing that I could see well enough to continue slowly and carefully. After all, I wasn't getting any drier by remaining parked in the deluge like the rest of the traffic. I had to get to a safe haven: a place of refuge from the elements. I really needed to dry out and get a good night's sleep.

Those last three days of the trip were driven through the rain. That's when I learned the value of good leathers and wet weather gear. I remember standing in a motel lobby in Rockwood, Tennessee on the fourth night of the ride, soaked to the skin asking for a room. "No vacancy, sorry," said the night clerk. I was incredulous and pleaded with the clerk for a spare bed. A rather large puddle was forming around me in front of the reception desk as I pressed the clerk for a room. Southern hospitality prevailed, as a passerby took pity on this wretched wet being and offered the spare bed in his room. Seizing the opportunity and thanking him profusely, I dried out and got a good night's sleep. I had found my refuge and safe haven for the night due to the kindness and compassion of a considerate hotel guest. The rug in front of the reception desk where I had stood the previous night was still wet the next day when I left the motel on the final leg of the trip.

On day five of my sojourn, I was off and running for Bragg. It was my day of grace, my termination of leave. My leathers were still damp under my wet-weather gear, and it continued drizzling outside. Off we went into the mist, my scrambler and I. It was a full-court press all the way to our destination that day. North Carolina is a beautiful state, but I was not interested in the scenery as time was of the essence. If a soldier is late in returning from leave or in reporting for a new assignment, he is considered to be absent without leave, or AWOL. That is considered to be a court martial offense. The bike and I strained to get to the military base in Fayetteville. We arrived at Fort Bragg and I signed in one minute before midnight. The Honda Scrambler brought me to my destination safe and sound, but with no time to spare. Yet, we had arrived in one piece and within the legal limits of my leave time.

I found out the next day when I reported for the course that I was the senior officer and, therefore, the class leader. Needless to say that it was not the best way to make a first impression on my supervisor. He was miffed that I had not arrived a day earlier, even though I was not required to do so, and had no prior knowledge that I was to be the class leader. I made my amends and proceeded to lead the class to a successful course completion during its nearly two month duration. All was well.

There was only one drawback to having attended the Special Warfare Course: I was promoted to Major on the field exercise during the last week of training. That doesn't sound like a negative connotation, but Majors don't command "A" Detachments, the basic elements of Special Forces. Captains command these units. One's peers in Special Forces deem command experience at "A" Detachment level imperative. Therein lies the negative connotation. I would be relegated to a staff position or to command of a "B" Detachment, the next higher echelon controlling several "A" Detachments, as a Major. There were few actively engaged "B" Detachments in operation in Southeast Asia. There was only a slim outside chance of my getting command of a special project, direct action, composite detachment as a Major. Otherwise, it looked like staff work would by my regimen for the next few years. I would miss my chance at acquiring the most important Special Forces experience possible by not serving with an "A" Detachment. This missed opportunity was most unfortunate and would later prove to be a detriment. But that would be much later toward the end of my military career.

Six weeks after I arrived at Fort Bragg, I sold the Honda Scrambler to a soldier who just couldn't live without it. It was a new model and a beauty in his eyes. He kept pestering me to let him buy the bike from the moment he first saw it. It had served its purpose. Besides, I would soon finish the Special Forces Course, receive orders and proceed to Okinawa to join the 1st Special Forces Group. Thereafter, I was certain that I would be Southeast Asia bound and ready for war. And so the quest progressed.

Chapter Seven

Okinawa Bound

Preparation – Special Forces Training and TDY

I proceeded to Okinawa after graduating from the Special Warfare Course at Fort Bragg. Although it was an accompanied tour with family, it would be eight months before my family was allowed to proceed to Okinawa. Availability of government living quarters was the cause of the delay. Oh, yes, and the fact that I was in Southeast Asia on a temporary tour of duty (TDY) for five months also had something to do with it. I had no sooner arrived at Camp Kue, Okinawa, and reported to my assigned "B" Detachment in the 1st SFGA, than I was made part of a composite team for Project 404, a special mission. After preliminary planning and training, I was off again to Southeast Asia and the war. When that "bumpy ride" was completed, the army let me stay put for about a year-and-a-half at group headquarters staff in Okinawa.

Okinawa Assignment, Position Promotion and Staff Work

I was reassigned as the 1st SFGA Adjutant or S1, Personnel Staff Officer at Camp Sansone. My job was to take care of all policy matters and administrative actions regarding personnel and to maintain personnel records for the 1st SFGA. I worked directly for the command group, that is the 1st Group Commander, Deputy Commander and Executive Officer.

Needless to say, they kept me busy.

I finally got my family to Okinawa and into government quarters at Camp Kue. The long separation had put an additional strain on our marriage. Obvious cracks were forming. The kids went to school, the wife did what stay-at-home wives did and I went to work each day. Things were outwardly calm and seemed normal, but we were not communicating much. I spent a lot of time at work and on solo activities outside of work. With a desk job during that interval of my life, I needed some action and freedom from stress. These were not forthcoming from the home front. The obvious answer was, what else, but a motorcycle – my ultimate diversion.

Scrambles Racing and Stress Release at Kadina and Naha

There were two scrambles tracks nearby at Naha City and Kadina Air Force Base. A scrambles race is conducted on an irregular, but generally circular, dirt track that incorporates tight turns, sweeper curves, jumps, soft and hard-packed dirt, and straight-a-ways allowing bursts of speed followed by hard braking tight turns. All I needed was a sponsor and a bike to achieve the action and stress relief that were so sorely needed. I found both at the local Kawasaki shop in Sukiran. The shop owner, a fine local motorcyclist by the name of Sakamoto San, became my sponsor; a Kawasaki 175cc dirt bike became my new scrambler. I bought the bike new as a manufactured, out-of-the-box scrambler ready for the track. Practice was needed to perfect the skills required for scrambles racing. Off to the track at Kadina I went, weekend after weekend, to develop the techniques for good starts, smooth jumps, engine braking and skid-turn negotiations. I was ready to try my hand at some actual scrambles racing against live competition after getting the hang of these techniques. Sakamoto San was instrumental

58

in talking me through the techniques with useful tips. We discussed everything from starting and tracking positions to passing techniques and speed to control factors. Finally, we determined what modifications would enhance the bike's performance.

After a few races at Kadina and Naha, which introduced me to the world of scrambles racing, we drastically modified the bike. I sent the mill back to the states for a bore and rotary valve job. We replaced both front and rear suspension systems and gave the bike longer front- end travel and stiffer rear-end spring action. Other appropriate adjustments were made to the bike's gearing, sprockets and carburetion. We even mixed special fuels. I began placing in the scrambles after all these modifications were completed. Although I never took first place, there were a few second and third place finishes to my credit.

A highlight of those scrambles was the day I took a jump too fast at the Naha track and was unable to make the dogleg right turn to follow the track afterward. I inadvertently changed scrambles into hill climbing as I blasted up the face of a near vertical cliff, did a loop-de-loop in mid-air, and landed in a heap on the track at the base of the cliff. Needless to say, both bike and rider were rendered incapable of continuing with that race. Taking the jump too fast set me off balance on landing and made it impossible to negotiate the right turn at the base of the cliff. There was nowhere to go but straight ahead up the face of the cliff. Alas! All that goes up must come down, and so we did. Bike and rider succumbed to the force of gravity. Fortunately, the only major damage that resulted was to the rider's ego. Otherwise, a few things bent but nothing broke.

Another memorable event occurred at the Kadina track the day I took the second place trophy. That was the zenith of my scramble racing days. It was hot under the blazing Okinawa sun and there was little breeze. There was a substantial lineup of bikes in the race that day. I was near the pole position at the starting line. A Bultaco motorcycle a few bikes down the line was having trouble getting started. I recall the driver, a grizzled and stocky fellow, vigorously kick-starting the engine several times and twisting the wick to fire it up. He finally succeeded in his efforts to get the bike started and to keep the engine revving. He was the aggressive sort, and I knew his would be the bike to beat. We were all ready. Sweat beads formed on our faces, bike engines revved loudly, clouds of exhaust plumes and dust spewed into the air, then the starter flag dropped and off we went bolting like lightening from the starting line up the track to our scramble's destiny. What a fine day for a race it was as each rider jockeyed for position on the track. Each bent forward in the saddle with white-knuckled hands gripping fast to the handlebar, clutch and throttle controls. Nostrils flared and eyes were intent on gauging the next turn or jump to be encountered. Muscles tensed and adrenalin flowed as the riders strained to take the lead in the race. The pack of bikes stayed tight initially, but after numerous circuits of the track the field began to stretch out. Two bikes faltered and dropped out of the race. Another hit a jump too fast and flew off the track. I was in or near the lead until the final two laps. The Bultaco rider and I played tag throughout the scramble. I would overtake him; he would overtake me. All the other bikes were behind us by the last few laps. Toward the end of the race the Bultaco 200cc Scrambler pulled ahead and increased its lead substantially until the final turn. I took the final jump and landed too close to the side of the track in loose dirt, which almost put me down and slowed the bike momentarily. Going into the final acute turn, about 30 yards from the finish line, the lead bike's engine died. The bike was at a dead stop in the apex of the curve. The driver had a substantial lead and was jabbing the kick-starter furiously as I came barreling into the turn, skidding into a position adjacent and parallel to the lead bike as its engine burst into life. Both bikes blasted to the finish line neck-and-neck. The 200cc Bultaco turned on like a screaming banshee; my 175cc Kawasaki fell one-half a wheel-length behind as we crossed the finish line in the face of a boisterous crowd. What a rush! I lost the race, but it was still a second place finish and a thrilling one at that. I complimented the Bultaco rider and couldn't help but admire his skill and, especially, his tenacity. He was a winner.

My second place finish elated me. It was a great race. Even my kids enjoyed watching their father race that day and take the second place trophy. It was one of the few times the wife brought them to the scrambles, and it was much appreciated. It remains a positive and memorable event. I have preserved the trophy in a place of honor to this day. Even Sakamoto San beamed his approval and basked in the glory of his Kawasaki motorcycle-shop sponsorship. After all, there were no Bultaco motorcycle dealerships on Okinawa. All was well with the world on that day. Just think of how the winner must have felt. His grail wasn't far off.

Although I didn't know it at the time, this was to be my last race in Okinawa. A new project awaited me at work the following week. Planning started for a huge special warfare joint, combined, bilateral exercise. It was to be conducted in a few months time on the Island of Taiwan with Republic of China Special Warfare Forces. I had to resource Exercise Forward Thrust I with hundreds of Army Special Forces personnel of all grades and occupational specialties. This was in addition to our 1st SFGA operational missions in Southeast Asia, and in particular, to our combat deployments in Vietnam. The Group was stretched to the limit to fill the requirements for Forward Thrust. The 1st Group Deputy Commander had to weigh in on forcing subordinate commanders to comply with the personnel levies from their units for the exercise. I even had to put myself on as the Assistant Chief Administrative Officer for the exercise and find a temporary replacement Adjutant for the remnant of the 1st SFGA during the interim. That's how critical the personnel picture became for the 1st SFGA during the exercise preparation phase in late 1968. We deployed to Taiwan on the 23rd of February, 1969 for five months worth of Exercise Forward Thrust I.

Our families were not happy about the deployment, but they were used to such events. Military families, especially Special Forces families, steel themselves against sudden, surprise assignments of their military spouses to places unknown for durations undetermined. Those family members left behind to keep the home fires burning banded together to help one another through the tough times of separation, loneliness and hardship. No wonder some of those families got worn out with the waiting, uncertainty and anxiety. Mine was one of those. My quest for the Holy Grail began to falter.

17. I enjoyed the camaraderie and pleasure of touring all over Japan with the Zama Motorcycle Club. (Nikko, Japan)

18. Life is sweet at a rest halt near Lake Ashino with Mount Fuji in the background. (The Skyline, Hakone, Japan 1983)

19. Comrades of the Camp Zama Motorcycle Club on the way to Mount Fuji. (Honshu, Japan 1984)

20. The horseless rider. Looks like the Black Ship took Bill Archer's bike. (ZMC Secretary at Hakone Park, Lake Ashino, Honshu, Japan 1984)

21. On the road climbing the foothills to the Japanese Alps. (Heading North in Honshu, Japan)

22. ZMC families in the vans; bikers on the bikes at a rest stop. (Somewhere in Japan, late 1985)

23. "My new Honda Saber 750cc did the trick for two-up riding with my wife." (Camp Zama, Japan 1986)

24. The Honda Saber 750cc handled well and was as smooth as silk with plenty of power. (Japan 1986)

25. Pit stop with Honda Saber 750cc. (Honshu, Japan 1986)

26. Dream Bike: The 1987 Kawasaki 750cc Ninja and admirer.
(Purchased in Kaiserslautern, Germany, June 1987)

27. "There are two things I remember most about the Kawasaki Ninja: speed and camaraderie." (Amy and Dad at Landstuhl, Germany 1987).

28. Park and walk on Easter Sunday tour in Luxemburg.
(Luxemburg 1987)

29. Summer in Japan on the way to Suwa Lake, and it's getting hot. (At left is Jack Owen, ZMC President, and Dennis Lid, Vice President)

30. Comaraderie: Going native on arrival in front of a Japanese Inn. (Left to right: Bi Yu Lid, Chuck Cash and Dennis Lid at Nikko 1990)

31. Final destination on last trip – Holy Family Mission, Saku, Japan. ("Call it an attack of spirituality: an urge to divest oneself of things… ")

Chapter Eight

Taiwan Sojourn

The Military Exercise – Forward Thrust I

On the five-month temporary duty tour to Taiwan for Exercise Forward Thrust I, I shipped the 175cc Kawasaki to Taipei, got a temporary license and used the bike for transportation to work and back to the guesthouse each day. Minor modifications had to be made to the bike prior to embarkation. Lights and a horn were added and a makeshift muffler was installed to make it street legal. Shipping the bike was an easy matter. The 1st Group Signal Officer and I were both motorcyclists. He had to transport the signal communication vans to the exercise, so we simply put our bikes inside the vans to hitch a ride. The vans were shipped by surface vessel in advance so as to arrive at the same time as the Group main body. The Taiwanese Police issued temporary motorcycle permits for our use upon arrival, since we were official participants of the exercise.

The lead element of the 1st SFGA landed by C-130 military cargo aircraft at Taipei International Airport during the late afternoon. The sky was a solid gray overcast; the weather was bleak and included a dismal drizzle. Things looked a bit foreboding. We were the advance party of the 1st SFGA. The rest of the Group would arrive over the next two days. The signal officer and I intercepted the signal vans and our bikes as soon as they arrived at the port within a couple days of our own arrival. We finally had "wheels."

Initially, our priority was to assign everyone to living quarters at the Eng Hsiang Guest House in a suburb of Taipei, then provide daily bus transportation to work and back for headquarters personnel. Our place of work was called "the tunnel." It was part of the actual defense network of tunnels used by the Army of Taiwan. The tunnels were in the mountains surrounding Taipei, Nationalist China's capital. Our Forward Thrust Exercise would cover the entire Island of Taiwan, also known as Formosa, from Ky Lung in the north to Ping Tung in the south. "The tunnel" was the exercise headquarters for the entire operation during its five month duration. Our bikes came in handy, especially during those first few days of set-up for the exercise. Contact, coordination and a myriad of tasks had to be accomplished during the preparatory phase just prior to exercise execution. The motorcycles gave us the means of getting from one place to another quickly and efficiently to conduct our business. They became an unplanned asset for us and for the exercise.

My boss on the exercise was a U.S. Navy Captain. He was an outstanding, hard-core officer with years of military and special warfare experience. He also knew how to lead, in that he was not a micro manager. The Captain gave his guidance and let me do the job, then checked progress along the way and the final results on mission accomplishment. One wing of the tunnel complex was mine, and all the S-1 Administrative Personnel occupied that wing. First Lieutenant Lew was my immediate assistant and a real workhorse. Our Non-Commissioned Officer-in-Charge (NCOIC) was a seasoned professional who made sure that the work was accomplished and that our Special Forces troopers were taken care of. We had established a smooth functioning organization to administer to the exercise participants. Forward Thrust commenced on time and ran its course to a successful conclusion. I was very proud of my people and the job they did on the exercise. They were adequately and justly rewarded for their efforts as well.

Soldiers are special and dedicated people who give much of themselves and ask for little in return. It's a funny thing, but I have also noted that a high proportion of them are attracted to the sport of motorcycling. Perhaps it is their sense of adventure or camaraderie that draws them to it. Whatever it is, there is a definite magnetism, and many of them make good motorcyclists too. Taipei brought out the best and worst in those of us bikers who were there.

The ride to work and back each day was a unique experience. Taipei traffic during 1969 was horrendous. Buses, trucks, taxicabs, cars, bicycles, motorcycles, scooters, carts and people were intertwined in a maze of chaotic imbroglio. What a mess! And it wasn't only at traffic times, but all the time. The worst offenders on the road were the taxicabs and dump trucks. Their opportunistic drivers seemed immune to the dangers around them and most had neither consideration nor respect for other drivers or their vehicles. They were the absolute, undisputed bullies of the road who created much of the chaos. Well, the signal officer and I targeted them specifically during our stay in Taipei. As much as was humanly possible, we did our best to scare the dickens out of them with our own hellish driving tactics. Sometimes it even worked. The looks on their faces revealed their astonishment, bewilderment and disbelief that anyone, especially a foreigner, would confront them with their own arrogant driving techniques. Our motorcycles won the day, initially, only because of their exhaust noise and surprisingly, unexpected maneuvers in confronting the bullies' bravado. Frankly, we were lucky that we weren't killed in giving them a "dose of their own medicine." So much for our stupidity and false pride in the face of such temptation. As an afterthought, the wiser and correct approach would have been to patiently and stoically endure like the rest of the victims. Keep the peace, brother, and know this: Your bike can't always speed or maneuver you out of harms way, so don't go there to begin with. Keep primal urges and road rage under control. Try to be a knight of the road. Oh words of wisdom, where are you when I need you? And hence, we contributed to the origin of the phrase, "The Ugly American."

Night Maneuvers – Downtown

We had time to enjoy the sights and relax during our time off from the exercise. Taipei was a tourist destination and a rest and relaxation point for our military service personnel, especially those stationed in Southeast Asia. Our gracious Chinese military hosts ensured that the exercise participants were treated with grand hospitality during our stay in Taiwan. They conducted several bilateral cultural and social events to establish good rapport with their counterparts from the American military. We were graciously toured, wined and dined on down time from the exercise.

It was at one of the social events that I met a certain young Chinese lady wearing a very becoming and tight-fitting, green Chinese dress called a cheongsam. She was the primary hostess of the social event held at a club in Taipei. There was no denying that she was extremely attractive in her beautiful Chinese dress, and spoke relatively fluent English as she welcomed us for the evening's festivities. Needless to say, she was the center of attention of the party participants all during the event. Her name was Bi Yu (pronounced: Bee Ye) meaning "Green Jade." Her figure was shapely and petite, her hair raven black caressing a beautiful oval face, her complexion was as smooth and clear as ivory, her eyes were elliptically shaped bright ebony pools and her enticing scarlet lips held an inviting smile. In later conversation, she informed

74

me that her family was of *Hakka* origin. *Hakka* is a people, a language dialect and a culture originating in Canton Province on Mainland China. The *Hakka* people are known for their honesty, hard work and fundamental simplicity. There is a basic purity about them that is intriguing. Bi Yu's family lived in Nan Chuang, Taiwan, a very small village three hours by bus to the south of Taipei. They owned and operated a small restaurant there. We struck up an immediate friendship, which would develop into much more than that in the future. An agreement made between the two of us at the party was that she would show me the sights in and around Taipei, if I would give her a ride on my motorcycle. The bargain was struck... and a lot more than that as time would tell.

My Hakka Gal and the Kawasaki Scrambler

When I had time off, I toured Taipei and the outskirts on my Kawasaki motorcycle. I took Bi Yu, the *"Hakka"* girl I met at the social event, on one of these excursions per our agreement. We took a ride up to Grass Mountain just north of Taipei riding tandem. That is, we rode two-up, one behind the other on the driver and buddy seats of the bike. I should have cautioned her in advance about what to wear. As it was, we bounced along two-up on the dirt road with her dressed in a blouse, mini-skirt and high heels, holding on behind me for dear life until we reached the top of the mountain. I thought it was great. It reminded me of entertainer Jackie Gleason's favorite expression, "How sweet it is." She, however, must have been scared to death. She did not want to go on another such ride. As I dropped her off at her sister's apartment in Taipei, she thanked me for the ride, and said that she hoped we would meet again. We had the good fortune of doing just that some weeks later.

One of the officers' rotated extra duties during the exercise

75

was to make a courier run down country to Ping Tung, the southernmost post on Forward Thrust I. We tried to make an operational visit and document exchange to the "A" Teams, or small detachments, along the way each month. The trip normally took two or three days to accomplish. I made the courier run about two-thirds of the way through the exercise with a Chinese Army driver and military pickup truck. The trip to Ping Tung with a few stops along the way to visit the detachments was relatively uneventful. The exception was a near miss by a very aggressive oncoming dump truck and driver. He owned the road and we were in his way. He ignored the fact that we were on his road and, as a result, we almost ended up in the ditch. A collision was avoided thanks to my driver's adroitness. The return trip was much more interesting.

Shortcuts are for people who know the area. I decided to take a shortcut through the mountains about halfway back to Taipei, somewhere in the vicinity of Taichung on the central coast of Formosa. I was motivated to do this because the village of Nan Chuang was located in the mountains along the route I had chosen. Nan Chuang was the town where Bi Yu and her parents lived. I thought I could save time by taking the shortcut, and that I might be able to visit Bi Yu and her parents along the way. It was an ill-conceived idea. Things aren't always what they seem to be on a map as compared to what they actually are on the ground, especially if the map is not current. As an aside, I wonder how many motorcyclists can testify to the truth of that statement. The result was that I ended up getting lost in those mountains, running out of asphalt road and using dirt trails and dead reckoning to find my way back to Taipei a day later than expected. On the positive side, I did find Nan Chuang, Bi Yu and her parents.

We drove into Nan Chuang at about 9 at night. By that time we should have been nearing Taipei. Well, we weren't going to get to Taipei that night. It was dark, and we were worn out from the day's navigating travails. I decided we would stay overnight wherever we could find accommodations in Nan Chuang. As it turned out, there was a decrepit, old inn across the street from Bi Yu's parent's restaurant and home. That looked like our best bet. I directed the driver to make the necessary arrangements at the inn for our overnight stay, as I needed his interpretation skills. With that task accomplished, I gave the driver the night off, told him we would depart for Taipei at 6 the following morning and to meet at the truck. I gave him some money to ensure he was taken care of for the night. Then I went to visit Bi Yu and meet her parents.

I wasn't sure if Bi Yu would be at her parent's place or in Taipei. My hope was that she was in Nan Chuang. When I walked into her parent's restaurant, I wasn't sure what to expect.

It was a small and simply decorated establishment on the ground floor of a three-story concrete and wood building with living quarters behind and above the restaurant. I took a seat at a table and proceeded to order some food with the elderly male waiter. My Chinese Mandarin language skills were very rudimentary, and I was having difficulty expressing my culinary desires to the waiter. As I was pondering what to say, I picked up the aroma of a familiar perfume. Bi Yu had entered the restaurant from the kitchen and was standing next to my table. She smiled and said in English:

"Hello Dennis. Good to see you. How did you get here and how may I help you?"

All of a sudden everything was fine. The elderly waiter turned out to be her father and the cook in the kitchen, her mother. There was an immediate rapport between all of us. The meeting, the meal and the visit were enjoyable and delightful but altogether too brief. I invited Bi Yu to dinner in Taipei the next time she visited her sister and before the exercise ended. After a short and restless night at the inn, the driver and I were on our way to Taipei – with a truckload of watermelons.

My Chinese driver had purchased watermelons with the money I had given him the previous night. He insisted that he could triple the money by selling the melons in Taipei. Thoughts of illegitimate use of a military vehicle and possible collusion entered my mind. I swallowed hard, divorced myself from any affiliation with his endeavor, and acknowledged his right to exercise the age-old Chinese practice of pragmatism to improve his lot. Letting it go at that, we arrived in Taipei that afternoon. The watermelon episode fortunately passed without further incident. I hoped, for my driver's sake, that it was a profitable and clandestine effort.

The end of Exercise Forward Thrust I came quickly. Work was fast-paced, time-sensitive and crushingly excessive during those final exercise days. We worked frantically to conclude our business at "the tunnel," phase out the exercise, ship our bikes in the vans, and prepare ourselves for the return trip to Okinawa. The mission was accomplished.

Our last night in Taipei was party time. I briefly attended the bilateral good-bye party with our Chinese counterparts. Then I bid a courteous but early adieu. Thereafter, I proceeded to meet Bi Yu at a quaint restaurant not far from the Eng Hsiang Guest House. I had arranged this rendezvous through her sister in Taipei. It was the fulfillment of the dinner invitation I had previously extended to Bi Yu in Nan Chuang.

As we enjoyed our meal, it was obvious to both of us that our friendship had grown to a point of intimacy. Our feelings for one another had grown strong and deep. I envisioned then, that the final result of our relationship would be tantamount to a tragic fall from grace. I shuddered at the thought and wondered how this matter could be resolved with any dignity at all. I told her that I would like to see her again, although I had no right to do so. She concurred that she would like that as well. When and how would be problematic and we left it to the future. Our parting afterward was in the words of Shakespeare: " ...such sweet sorrow."

Thereafter, I returned to Okinawa and sold the bike, then went on a final one-year tour of duty to Vietnam and the war, an experience in itself. It was like a trip to Dante's Inferno and seemed to be an eternity in hell. I often thought the punishment was like a self-inflicted wound. My internal moral compass had gone haywire; I had lost sight of the Holy Grail.

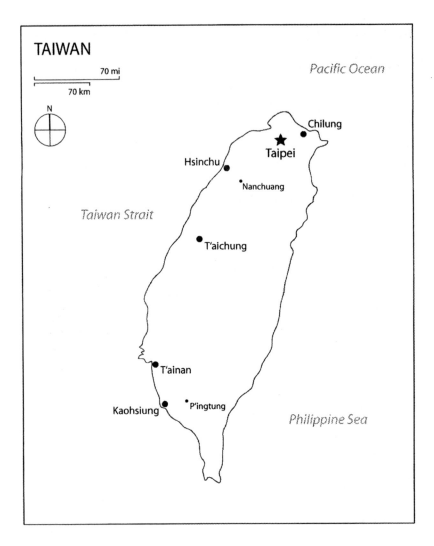

Taiwan Map

Chapter Nine

Years Of Drought

Last Tour to Vietnam

Orders from the Department of the Army awaited me upon my return to Okinawa from Exercise Forward Thrust I. They were for a one-year combat tour of duty to Vietnam, again, this time with the 5th Special Forces Group. I would ultimately be assigned to Military Assistance Command, Studies and Observations Group (MACSOG). The orders didn't specify that this was also known as a Special Operations Group, but that's the truth of the matter. These Special Forces troopers were the elite of the elite in Southeast Asia. They ran highly classified special operations missions in their area of operations. Their risk factor was high; their life expectancy was short. Without exaggeration, the men on the special operation teams lived a life of danger. So into the cauldron I went, but there were things to be done before departing for war.

The wife was not happy about the orders. My going off to war again, along with my fall from grace, was the last straw. Her recent romantic interests lay elsewhere as well. By mutual agreement we decided to separate and pursue a divorce while I was in Vietnam. The kids would go with the wife. Our fractured marriage was broken beyond repair this time, and the sham would soon be at an end – so much for our marriage vows. It reminds one of the popular song *Doesn't Anybody*

Stay Together Anymore by Phil Collins.

I took the bike to Sakamoto's Kawasaki shop in Sukiran, Okinawa, arranged to sell the motorcycle through him for whatever price he could manage and said my good-byes. He would take a small commission and send a check to me for the balance. He was good for his word, as I received payment four months later while in Vietnam. He was, indeed, a true friend and a fine motorcyclist who will always be remembered. I hated to part with that bike as well. It was the one I owned when I met Bi Yu, the one on which we went to Grass Mountain in Taiwan. I owed that introduction to my Kawasaki 175.

We packed the furniture and shipped it out along with the family members. I wrapped up my remaining Okinawa duties and took leave in Taiwan on the way to my new Vietnam assignment. While on leave, I promised Bi Yu that if I lived through the Vietnam tour, I would return to Taiwan and to her. Then it was off to war.

In one way it was a relief; in another way it was stressful. War in Vietnam and the unknown future created mixed feelings. Idealism evoked positive thoughts and emotions of helping to keep the Vietnamese people and all Southeast Asians free from Communism. Pragmatism and practicality, especially in view of President Nixon's declaration of "Vietnamization," elicited conflicting ideas and sentiments. Why should we continue to fight if, in the long run, we intended to throw in the towel and walk away from the war? Things didn't make much sense in late 1969 and through 1970 in Southeast Asia. Everything regarding the war seemed to be upside down. We fought on hoping for the best but fearing the worst. My country's loss of honor, its fall from grace, seemed to coincide with my own. Signs of failure were written in the wind. We had signaled our willingness to withdraw. Failure and loss were politically preordained and, therefore, inevitable.

I agonized through the year, first in training for Launch Site Commander at Quan Loi, then as the S3 Operations Officer of Command and Control South (CCS) in Ban Me Thuot, and finally as the Executive Officer of Command and Control North (CCN) of DaNang. Through it all I made two fateful decisions and took the necessary actions accordingly. Filing for divorce was followed by my resignation request from commissioned, active duty military service. It was the double whammy! The failure of my marriage, the war and its preordained, programmed, political failure, inability to get an assignment to Taiwan after Vietnam, thoughts of Bi Yu, chaos and disorder in my professional and personal life led me to make these decisions and to take these detrimental and irreversible actions. It seemed like a deliberate path to self-destruction. Clear thinking was certainly not the order of the day, except with regard to my immediate military duties. I crossed the Rubicon and there was no looking back.

Shaken but alive, I completed my final Vietnam tour of duty. I returned to the United States and honorably resigned from the army relinquishing my regular army commission but retaining my inactive reserve commission as an army major. Since I had completed over ten years of active duty commissioned service, I retained tenure. My divorce was also granted. Then I went back to Taiwan as a civilian and married my little *Hakka* gal. Thirty-five years of bliss with Bi Yu testify to the fact that it was the best thing I ever did. She was and is my saving grace. Our marriage was a simple civil ceremony by the judge at the Taipei Court. Many years later we were re-married in a religious ceremony by the church, after an annulment was granted for my first marriage. Danny and Amy, our two children, were sitting in the front pew as witnesses along with a couple of strangers. How convoluted life can be. Confused? So am I.

If one works overseas for and is sponsored by one's own

government, or an international corporation, all is well. If not, one takes on high risks. Mine was a solo, un-sponsored status as a civilian during the one-year stay in Taiwan. I was at risk. The shipping company with which I was employed was dependent on the success of a joint venture proposal with a Chinese firm. The proposal failed to materialize into an actual joint venture. The shipping company's demise was imminent. My job as an assistant manager would be terminated as a result. I opted for an immediate return to active military service through Military Assistance and Advisory Group (MAAG), China. But there was another problem. The personnel draw down from Vietnam had commenced as well. Officers were not being hired: they were being fired. If I wanted to return to army active duty service, my only alternative was to enlist. That's what I did. I became what is known as a dual component soldier. That is, I was a commissioned officer as a major in the inactive reserve and a non-commissioned officer as a sergeant on active duty. I remained on active duty for the next nine-and-a-half years as a non-commissioned officer in the army, eventually rising to the rank of sergeant first class (SFC). Because of my tenure as a major, I retired in 1980 at the highest grade held on active duty. I retired as a U.S. Army Major. Still confused? You've got company.

Peacetime in Hawaii with My Worst Bike

My assignments as a sergeant in the army were in Hawaii with the 25th Infantry Division (25th ID) working in brigade operations; then at the 25th ID Non-commissioned Officers' Academy as a RECONDO (Reconnaissance) Commando Instructor; and later, for one year, as a U.S. Army Recruiter; then finally as a Special Forces trooper in Panama. After the passage of these assignments and nine-and-a-half years, I retired from the army with almost 21 years of total active duty service.

I owned only one motorcycle during all my time as a U.S. Army Non-commissioned Officer. During those years served with the 25th ID in Hawaii at the RECONDO Course, I owned a Yamaha 250cc Scrambler. It was old, used and highly abused. That's the way I bought it from another soldier who was rotating to the mainland for his next active duty assignment. He needed the cash more than the bike; I wanted the bike more than the cash. The Yamaha 250cc, single cylinder dirt bike never did run right even after spending time and money trying to rehabilitate it. The bike reminded me of some muscle bikes; it looked good but handled like a dog. Yet, it did the job of running the dirt roads on East Range in the Koolau Mountains of Oahu, Hawaii, where I worked as an instructor at the commando course. This was the only bike I was ever glad to be rid of. It wasn't the make or model that made it so; it was the initial abused condition, which I could not correct. Some problems just can't be rectified. I sold that Yamaha prior to attending the Non-commissioned Officers' Advanced Course at Fort Benning, Georgia, then the Spanish Language School in Monterey, California, in preparation for my final assignment to Panama with the 3/7th Special Forces Battalion.

Active Duty Finale in Panama with No Bike

The two good things derived from the Panama assignment were the replacement of the family I had lost through my previous divorce and honorable retirement as a major from the active army.

Bi Yu had given birth to our son, Daniel, in Hawaii and our daughter, Amy, in the Canal Zone. Panama ushered in the completion of our new family, which replaced and added to the

85

old one. My two children from the first annulled marriage, Debby and Charlie, were still part of my family even though they were older, on their own and far away. Such blood ties cannot be broken even by time, distance or temporary estrangement. It was good that the family was finally restored.

I arrived in Panama and Camp Gulick on the Caribbean side of the isthmus with the idea that this would be my last active army assignment. Retirement three years hence was my goal. I was after my pound of flesh. Normally a tour of duty with the U.S. Army Special Forces anywhere in the world would be cause for celebration, as it was with the 3/7 SFGA. Only this celebration was muted because it came so late in my career. I just wasn't "gun ho" anymore. Twice I had tried to regain my officer's commission on active duty, and twice it was denied. "Others were found to be more outstanding," quoted the denials from Headquarters, Department of the Army. So be it! I contented myself with trying to be the best sergeant in the army for several years throughout my non-commissioned service. At times I succeeded; at other times I failed to live up to that expectation. With the completion of my final tour of duty in Panama, it was time to retire, regain my commissioned title of major and collect my pound of flesh.

After concluding my last assignment in Panama without a bike, I retired from the army and went to work in Hawaii for eight months. It took that much time to process for a position with the Department of Defense as a civilian in Japan working specifically for, guess whom... the army. The fall from grace was on the mend for both country and fallen patriot. The search for the Holy Grail resumed.

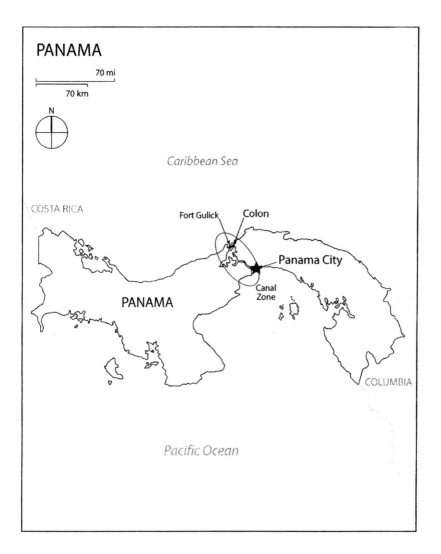

Panama Map

Chapter Ten

Fresh Start

Japan Civilian Venture

Our family's fresh start as civilians on the Japan venture was a great 18-year experience with the Department of Defense that included a one-year hiatus to Europe for a special project. We lived outside the Camp Zama Army Base on the Japanese civilian economy initially. The base was the Headquarters for U.S. Army Japan and IX Corps located thirty kilometers south of Tokyo. It was the primary American Army base in Japan and was my place of work, first as a Management Analyst, then as a Military Exercise and Plans Specialist. Our house was a Japanese-style wooden structure and was very small and basic by American standards. It was difficult to heat and cool because it was of single-wall construction and leaked air like a sieve. We managed with the marginal housing using army quartermaster furniture and learned to make do with the limited space and other inconveniences. We gained a few Japanese friends from the neighborhood in the process of living there. Three years later we moved on base and occupied military officer quarters. What a pleasant difference. We finally acquired American-standard housing on base. It was like living in an American colony within a Japanese society. We had all the positive aspects of living overseas with none of the negative points. Life was good.

The Honda Cruising and Touring Years

Motorcycling provided stress relief for me just as golf or some other sport might relieve the pressure of work for others. We all have our own way of relaxing and recharging. I owned three bikes at separate times during those years of cruising, touring and casual road racing while stationed at Camp Zama. The first was a Honda CX-500cc general-purpose cruising bike. It was a rabbit-ear, twin-cylinder, water-cooled touring bike, and a dependable and willing mount at that. I enjoyed the comfort of the upright sitting position for low-speed touring and cruising. However, at high speed without a windscreen, it was a constant battle to counter the wind resistance. Fortunately, this was only a problem on the expressways in Japan and not on the secondary roads, where most of our touring was accomplished. It was while I owned this bike that I joined the Camp Zama Motorcycle Club (ZMC) and enjoyed the camaraderie as well as the pleasures of touring all over Japan from the northern island of Hokkaido, throughout the main island of Honshu, where Camp Zama was located near Tokyo, to the southern island of Kyushu. The CX-500 was smooth and capable on the long, lazy curves descending from the Skyline at Hakone National Park to the Kanto Plain and low hills of Sagamihara and Camp Zama. I remember keeping time to the music of my portable tape recorder as our troop of bikes from the club undulated from left to right through those sweeping curves. It was like the music was written for riding that particular road, and the bike and I were dancing to the tune.

One experience on the CX-500 that I recall vividly was something that I feel must be related to my fellow motorcyclists as a cautionary note. I do not wish this particular incident on anyone. You all know what a fixed-bubble face shield is, don't you? It's a clear, plastic, fish-bowl-like

89

facemask affixed to the helmet that protects the face and eyes from the elements and road debris. The fixed variety snaps on to the front of the helmet and does not swivel upwards but remains fixed in front of the face. These face shields should not be worn while riding if you have a cold or like to chew tobacco. Now I don't chew, but once, when I had a cold and without thinking, I made the mistake of forgetting that I was wearing the bubble face shield. I spat as I turned my head to the side while riding my bike at 55 mph. Panic! The spittle hit the plastic bubble with a splat and scattered all over the inside of the face shield. You never saw a bike stop so fast in all your life. Well, I hope you get the idea. Beware of the bubble face shield.

The CX-500 was a willing and dependable cruiser but not quite able with regard to speed and torque. After three years of ownership, it was time to upgrade to a more powerful machine. I sold the CX 500cc and bought a Honda Saber 750cc touring motorcycle. The 750 cubic centimeter engine seems to be the most versatile. It is very powerful, usually four cylinder in configuration, compact and relatively lightweight that fits snuggly into a medium weight cradle or frame. This assembled combination creates a motorcycle with a very favorable horsepower to weight ratio. Such a bike is the ultimate in speed, maneuverability, efficiency and functional design. It is the model of the optimum motorcycle. Going above the 750cc class of bike is too heavy; going below it is too light. Staying at 750cc is just right (according to Lid's Law).

We did a lot of two-up riding in the ZMC. Husbands and wives, boyfriends and girlfriends enjoyed touring on weekends with the club. Even the kids came by van provided by adult club members so that the whole family could enjoy these weekend sojourns. My new Honda Saber 750cc did the trick for two-up riding with my wife. It was a great touring bike with its long wheelbase, shaft drive, windscreen, and bulletproof

V-four engine. It handled well and was as smooth as silk with plenty of power and torque. It served us well on the long, overnight weekend rides to various destinations in Japan. This bike took us through a rather harrowing experience on one of our trips. We drove through a typhoon. Several of the club's bikes flooded out and had to stop for servicing before continuing. The carburetors, air cleaners, gas tanks and brake pads had to be flushed, cleaned and dried to eliminate the water. The Saber sputtered a few times but continued to function efficiently through the typhoon and into the sunshine beyond. We stopped to dry out after going through the mountain pass, out of the typhoon's path and into the valley beyond. The few years of ownership of the Saber ended when I was assigned to Europe on a special project for one year. I sold the bike and moved the family to Europe.

The European Aberration and Dream Bike Acquisition

After getting settled in Landstuhl, Germany, and going to work on the concept plans project at Panzer Kasern near Kaiserslautern, I began the search for my dream bike. I had always wanted a BMW motorcycle. This was my chance. Yet, after visiting several BMW dealerships, I decided against it. The "Beamers" are beautifully crafted and well-made bikes, yet they are heavy, bulky and somewhat awkward looking. They are also very expensive. As I searched for that dream bike, I compared the BMWs with the Japanese bikes and decided to purchase the Kawasaki 750R. The 1987 Ninja was beautiful in design, high-tech, compact, complete with full-body fairing or shell, powerful with its vertical four-cylinder engine, excellent in braking and adequate in suspension. Its horsepower-to-weight ratio was perfect; its cost-to-benefit ratio was ideal. It probably would not last as long as the BMW, but it would definitely outlast me. It was my dream bike.

There are two things I remember most about the Kawasaki Ninja: speed and camaraderie. I put it to the speed test on the Autobahn from Kaiserslautern, Germany, to Innsbruck, Austria. I wanted to see if the bike could reach its advertised 137 mph top-end. On a stretch of level road near Munich, I went into a full tuck and opened up the throttle. The turbine smooth vertical-four swiftly moved the bike past the 100 mph mark. I was amused at the fast moving Mercedes and BMW automobiles well in front of me that were moving over to the slow lane just to see what kind of motorcycle (or maniac) was closing the distance behind them so quickly. I felt like I was flying when I hit 120 mph. By the time I reached 130, there was a distinct feeling of skittishness or instability. I still had throttle left at 135 mph but declined to press it any further. The bike could definitely do the claimed top-end, but this driver had reached his limit. As I backed off the throttle and rose up slightly out of the full tuck position, the wind resistance on my helmet, chest and elbows rapidly reduced the speed to less than 110 mph. I brought the bike down to a speed of 85 and cruised the rest of the way to Innsbruck, passing through the mountain border crossing at two in the morning and arriving at the destination about an hour later. Needless to say, that ride provided a real adrenalin rush. It would be followed by a few more such rides before completing the special project in Europe and returning to Asia.

During the short-lived European assignment of about one year, the special project at work, the search for my Kawasaki 750cc Ninja dream bike and my family were the focal points of my life. I completed the concept plans project, found and purchased my dream motorcycle, my wife became a convert to the faith and my children continued their education while stationed at Landstuhl, Germany. What more could a man ask for? All was well with life. I rode on occasion with motorcyclist friends to Luxembourg, throughout Germany and

Austria. The scenery was breathtaking, the weather extremely and rapidly changeable and the experiences were adventuresome and exhilarating. I did not join any of the German motorcycle clubs, although I rode with one for a short time. There simply was too little time to become involved.

My second fond memory of the 750cc Ninja was experienced in Japan over the next six years. It was that of camaraderie in riding with The Camp Zama Motorcycle Club of Sagamihara (Camp Zama), Japan. Whether our club rides were with a few bikes on a long trip or many bikes on a short trip, they were just plain fun. We certainly scratched the back of the main islands of Nippon from Hokkaido in the North to Kyushu in the South. The Japanese Alps on Honshu have some of the best knee-dragging, gut-wrenching, curvy mountain roads I've ever driven. The scenery was spectacular, the company superb and the whole experience was a pure delight. Camaraderie drew me closer to where my treasure lay. I pursued the grail with greater alacrity and zeal.

Germany Map

Chapter Eleven

Return To Japan

The special project working on concept plans for the 21st Support Command at Panzer Kasern in Kaiserslautern, Germany lasted for eleven months. Then my supervisor at Camp Zama requested that I return to Japan to continue work in the G3 Exercise Plans Division on Overseas Deployment Training and Exercise Plans issues. One of the G3 specialists in this area of expertise had transferred to Okinawa and the G3 Exercise Operations Officer needed me back in Japan. So off I went with the family to Headquarters, U.S. Army Japan/IX Corps at Camp Zama and my job as an Exercise and Military Plans Specialist. I was happy to comply, as I had spent most of my career in the Orient and considered myself to be an Asia hand more than a European hand. It was simply my preference.

The Kawasaki Ninja Experience

The family settled down in government quarters at Zama very quickly. It was an easy relocation because we were already familiar with the base and with Japan. It was good to be back with our old acquaintances and business associates. Even my 750cc Kawasaki Ninja motorcycle seemed to be at home, which, indeed it was. After all, the "rice cooker" was of Japanese origin, though I purchased it in Germany through the Canadian Post Exchange (military store). Driving on the left-hand side of the road took a little getting used to after growing accustomed to driving on the right-hand side in Europe. Contending with the narrow roads, dense traffic conditions and Kanji road signs also required greater concentration when driving. It was time to adapt to new surroundings again. That's what keeps life interesting.

I got back into the swing of things on the job with G3 as an Exercise Plans Specialist at Camp Zama and stayed busy with work. Relaxing and relieving tension from work was not a problem. I had rejoined the Camp Zama Motorcycle Club (ZMC). The club became my tension reliever, as it was before I left Japan for Germany a year earlier. Returning to the ZMC was like coming back to family. I felt like I was at home again. After I took the motorcycle safety course and acquired my USARJ/Japanese Motorcycle License, I was ready to roll on weekend rides.

The first such ride was to a particular rest stop along the Chuo Expressway. It was next to a Sea of Japan beach on the Kanto Plain of Honshu Island. This rest area was a meeting place, a gathering point for tourists and motorcyclists on the way to the Izu Peninsula. The Japanese motorcycle club riders and others congregated there on weekends to mingle and swap yarns. It was one of the ZMC's favorite rest stops. The newest manufactured and custom motorcycles, accessories, gear, gadgets and riding attire could be observed there along with their owners. New friends were made and interesting discussions and demonstrations ensued. The language barrier proved to be no obstacle with the common denominator of the bike as the basis for   discussion and the focal point of attention. Words, phrases, sign language, body language and a common love of motorcycling filled in the gaps of understanding. The knights of the road were together, and that's all that mattered.

The Camp Zama Motorcycle Club

On that first ride to the rest stop after returning to Japan, my thoughts were immersed in a reverie of the origins and history of the Zama Motorcycle Club. As I stood watching the other riders at the rest stop, vaguely cognizant of their murmurings in the background, my thoughts flashed back to the birth and life of our ZMC.

In the beginning was the bike, and the bike was with rider, and the rider formed the club. Not long ago on the Kanto Plain in the Land of the Rising Sun an entity was born. It was in the form of a motorcycle club that does honor to all aficionados of the two-wheeled conveyance. That unique organization was known as the Camp Zama Motorcycle Club (ZMC). As I stood there mesmerized in my fantasy, I realized, with a cold chill running up my spine, that the day would come when the ZMC would be no more. I wanted, more than ever, to keep it alive as we roamed the highways and byways of Japan and to be a permanent part of its memory upon its demise. My reverie lingered on as I thought back to the club's early days.

The club founder's first name is Larry, an African American soldier formerly stationed in Japan, whose last name is lost in the shadows of history. He was a Harley rider and a wild seed, but he loved to ride. He, and fellow riders of the same ilk and with the same brand of bikes, founded the ZMC during 1978. It was established as a private association and was chartered and sanctioned by the U.S. Army Garrison Honshu Commander and U.S. Army Japan/IX Corps at Camp Zama, Japan. The camp is located thirty kilometers south of Tokyo at Sagamihara in Kanagawa Prefecture on the Kanto Plain of the main island of Honshu. The common thread that brought these folks together was their love of motorcycling. Recognition by camp officials authorized them the use of garrison facilities, including an old wooden building at Sagami Depot some thirty

97

minutes' drive from Zama. This building became their clubhouse and repair facility. The original members equipped it with salvaged furnishings, workbenches and a pool table. This facility served the members well during the club's nearly fifteen years of existence. The club logo and colors were displayed within the clubhouse and embroidered on the vests worn over our jackets or leathers. The original logo, ZMC letters connecting white wings, was later changed to the U.S. Stars and Stripes and Japanese Rising Sun encircled with appropriate inscriptions to complete our colors. Larry and the early members initiated all these things and bequeathed them to their successors. As the years passed and new members joined, the character and texture of the club changed as well. In my mind's eye, I dwelt on thoughts of how the club had changed.

The diverse membership of the ZMC over the years led to the rise of the "rice cooker," the Japanese motorcycle, as their machine of choice. This preference changed the character of the club from a "Harleyesque" nature to an international texture along with an altered image. The maverick image mellowed to a gentler, more organized and disciplined image. Instead of a rough tool, the club honed itself into a fine precision instrument as roving ambassadors of goodwill for the U.S. and Japan. As truckers in the states used to be, the ZMC riders evolved into true "knights of the road." Led by men like Dave Newman, club president during 1982/83, Harry New, his road captain and army civilian employee at Sagami Depot, Vice-President Glen Keener, an intelligence detachment civilian employee, Treasurer Dan Reyes, a Non-commissioned Officer with Garrison Honshu and Secretary Bruce Lucas, the club refined its constitution, bylaws and developed a group riding guide (rules of the road for formation flying). Club officers inspected the appearance of bike, rider and equipment prior to each ride. We were briefed on route, destination address, telephone numbers and emergency procedures. We rode according to the rules but took advantage of every legal loophole, such as split-lane driving and curb crawling. We used the staggered formation on group rides and arm, hand and light signals to convey commands to the formation. Dave Newman once said that our club was unique because, "Its riders would ride anytime, anywhere, during any weather [including typhoons]." Glen Keener noted that the uniqueness of equality extended to all ranks, military and civilian, all races, religions and nationalities. It was a level playing field for all concerned, and that's what made it "a great club." The club included military and civilian members and was bilateral in that we had both Japanese and U.S. members; it was multi-racial and ecumenical multi-denominational; it was a harmonious melting pot that defied the ugly American image and was a living example of tolerance and the golden rule. Keener was fond of saying, "It ain't only where we're goin', it's how we get there that's important." He enforced this doctrine during his reign as president, vice-president and later, as road captain. The list of abiding club members was an illustrious one that included men and women from various units and agencies. They drove a multitude of different motorcycles, models and displacements from Yamaha to Honda and Suzuki to Kawasaki. Some of these riders are mentioned herein by name; my apologies are offered to those worthy folks who are not.

Camaraderie and Sport Touring in the Land of Nippon

My recollections of the ZMC continued unabated as I recalled that we rode according to an annual schedule developed by Harry New, Ken Hirano and others. Our shortest motorcycle trips were day rides to nearby areas such as Yamanaka and the five lakes region at the foot of Mount Fuji during June, Hakone National Park and Lake Ashi in October, the beach on the Sea of Japan for New Year's sunrise, and a

99

family picnic along the river at Tanzawa Prefecture Park during May. Our longest trips included a seven-day journey to Kyushu, the southern island of Japan, and a nine-day venture to Hokkaido, the northern island. These excursions required ferryboat rides across the straits. Two members who enjoyed these long rides were Jack Owen and Chuck Cash. Both of these bigger-than-life individuals were dynamic and charismatic presidents, road captains or other club officials during the mid to late 80's and early 90's. Both were Japanese linguists. Jack, a Lieutenant Colonel in the intelligence detachment, was the quiet intellectual type and our chief navigator. Charlie, an army Master Sergeant in intelligence, was our colorful and flamboyant point man on the rides. He rode by the seat of his pants and dead reckoning. Both were excellent riders. We knew when it was time to assume formation and move because of Charlie's "on the road again" exhortation. Jack advised that we follow his navigational instructions by reminding us "we rode with our hearts, while he rode with his head." Then off we would go on one of our many overnight rides to Suwa Lake during May, gateway to the Japanese Alps and home to one of the best minshukus (Japanese inn) in Japan, or Shimoda in June with its white sands beaches and Black Ship on the Izu Peninsula, or Nikko through Tokyo to the mountains and the famous Kegon Falls and Chuzenji Lake in September. There were weekend trips to Hida-Takayama in the Japanese Alps during October to view the change of seasons, the Chiba Peninsula in November with its great bikers' roads, the strawberry picking run to Shizuoka in February, the Fertility Festival at Inuyama (Nagoya) during March and the cherry blossom viewing trip to Okutama Lake during April. We took other trips to various destinations during the year. Besides the joy of riding, despite dense traffic in the urban areas of the Kanto Plain, the narrow roads, the deep benjo ditches (gutters) adjacent to the roadside, the detours due to mudslides or washed out bridges in the mountains, the wind and rain of typhoons or sleet and snow of winter storms, we were "knights of the road" and roving ambassadors on all our rides. That is what made us proud to be members of the ZMC. We made friends along the way, which added to the joy of riding. I breathed deeply and sighed contentedly as I remembered all these things and allowed my visualizations of the ZMC to proceed uninterrupted.

The enjoyment continued with our overnight stops at the minshukus that rented Japanese-style rooms, provided meals and bathing facilities to travelers. We'd top-off our tanks at the end of the day, wash and park our bikes, and head for the "Ofuro" (Japanese style bath). Nothing felt better than a steaming hot communal bath to sooth sore muscles and swap yarns at day's end. Then we would eat, drink and sing karaoke music until we felt no pain. Thereafter, we crawled into our futon beds and slept soundly 'till dawn, when we awoke, ate and were soon on the road again. If it were a Sunday, we tried to find religious services for those who wanted to attend. That was no mean task in a country that is only two percent Christian. Many times, Jack (Mormon), Chuck (Catholic) or Glen (Protestant) would pilot our would-be worshipers (all denominations) to the right church if one could be found along our route. This is what made the club tolerant and ecumenical. It was during one of these quests that the ZMC discovered a small Franciscan mission at Saku, Japan, attended services, and established a tradition that lives on to this day. The tradition is the Thanksgiving Day meal celebrated at the mission. Each Thanksgiving Day since the ZMC discovered the mission and met Father Gabriel Alba, a Columbian Catholic Priest of the Franciscan Order, members of USARJ bring the makings up to Saku and prepare the meal to celebrate with the padre and his small staff. It is hoped that others will carry on this tradition of the ZMC as its legacy long after it closes its doors. My thoughts pursued other memories of the club's life as I stood pensively watching the others at the rest stop.

The club supported its members through two events held at Camp Zama each year. They were the 4th of July and Bon Odori (Japanese equivalent of All Souls Day). The ZMC operated a refreshment booth and gave motorcycle rides at these events. A percentage of the proceeds was paid back to the Camp Zama community while the remainder went into the club treasury. These events provided revenue to pay for bike trips, club bills, scholarships and other expenses during the year. Minshuku rental, expressway tolls or other costs for each trip were paid by the club. The rest was paid out of pocket by each rider. Funds were sufficient during the good years. I wondered how long the good years would last, as I concluded my historical review and reverie of the ZMC.

Our club riders were gathering together and starting up their bikes in the preliminaries to departure from the rest area. We shouted and waved our good-byes over the roar of engines as we made our way into ZMC riding formation. Slowly we weaved our way through the thick mob of people and bikes to finally break out onto the open road. Soon we were formation flying according to ZMC standing operating procedure. The creation of new experiences and memories and the building of a closer camaraderie between us would continue for a few more years to add to the club's history. Its rides and life would continue for a time longer, and lucky were we who were part of it all. Such memories would linger for a lifetime thereafter. Though still shrouded in mist, the vision of the grail grows more distinct.

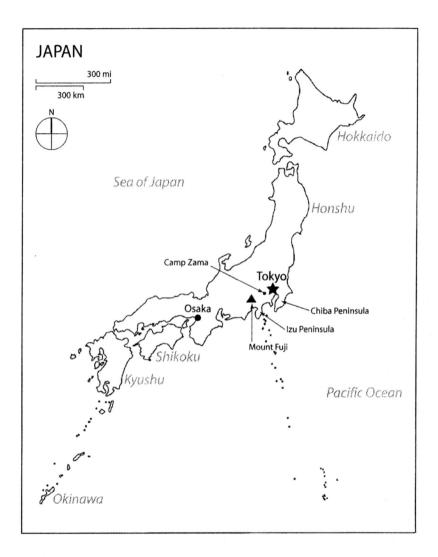

Japan Map

Chapter Twelve

Last Hurrah

The Gradual Demise of the ZMC

The bad years for the Zama Motorcycle Club (ZMC) started about 1990 when the Japanese economic bubble burst. The economy kept going downhill thereafter. The cost of bikes, insurance, road and ferryboat tolls, gasoline and minshukus (inns) increased due to an unfavorable dollar/yen exchange rate. Reassigned members left the club and returned to the States; few new riders joined. Club membership dropped from 42 bikes (about 55 family members) during the '80's to 12 bikes (about 18 family members) by '92. Only four or five riders of those who were left participated in club rides. Morale plummeted to an all time low.

I recall one of our final rides just prior to Vice President Charlie Cash's reassignment to the States. We started out for the rest area near the beach on the Sea of Japan where the local motorcyclists gathered, but we never arrived there. The coffee shop where we stopped for refreshment along the way was as far as we got. There was little conversation over our coffee. Each of us was steeped in thought and almost oblivious to our surroundings and to one another. Emotions were strong and rendered us deaf and mute. Charlie, always one of the club principals closest to its heart, was to leave in the next few days. We knew that his departure would signal the final demise of the ZMC. We got back on our bikes, looked at one another with vacant stares and without a word being said, turned around and headed home.

The declining economy, lack of funds, no new riders and low morale led to the end of the club by October of 1992. We took one final ride, conducted our termination meeting, closed the clubhouse doors for the last time and turned in the key for the ZMC. Once vibrant with life, the ZMC is now dead and gone. There are no monuments dedicated to it; there are few reminders that it ever existed. Its only legacy is the Thanksgiving Day dinner service at the Franciscan Mission in Saku, now provided by Camp Zama non-motorcyclist personnel. Yet, the memory of the ZMC lives on in the hearts and minds of its former members.

The Incident, Age Degradation, and an Attack of Spirituality

All good things must end. The end of my riding days came gradually over a period of months after the demise of the ZMC. One rainy night while returning on my bike from a weekend trip to Saku, Japan, I experienced a visual blackout. It only lasted for two or three seconds, but it was a scary incident. I literally could not see during that brief interval. It occurred at night, in the rain, at 50 mph on a downhill run coming out of the foothills and onto the coastal plain near Nirasaki, Japan. The cause of the visual aberration was unknown. Even a visit to the doctor after the trip didn't shed any light on the "why" of it all.

After that blackout incident, I noticed that I was becoming more cautious and conservative in my driving. I also avoided riding at night, especially in the rain. Driving aggressively with full confidence became a thing of the past. Yes, one must drive defensively to be safe, but one must never lose that aggressive offensive spirit that keeps a biker out of trouble and permits the use of speed and maneuverability to get out of harm's way. Once that spirit is lost, you're "an accident waiting for someplace to happen." That's when wisdom tells you it's time to quit riding for good. Add age with its inherent reduced strength and stamina, slower reflexes and response times, and general physical and psychological degradation, and the mix results in the conclusion that it's time to "hang it up."

There was another ingredient as well. Call it an attack of spirituality, an urge to divest oneself of things, especially the most pleasurable things. Why would spirituality necessitate giving up something that brought a person pleasure or joy? It's all about sacrifice or self-deprivation to achieve something good. One diets to lose weight, engages in physical training to maintain good health or studies diligently to gain knowledge. "No pain equals no gain," as the saying goes. Sacrifice is the whole point of growing spiritually. Think of it as you would a Lenten practice to grow in sanctity. One gives up something that is legitimately pleasurable as a sacrifice, as an act of love for one's Creator, for the purpose of spiritual growth or holiness. It's a withdrawal from the material or temporal to advance toward the spiritual. Your treasure is where your heart is. It is not that spirituality necessitates giving up something that brings you pleasure or joy; it is that voluntary sacrifice of the pleasure or joy can yield growth in spirituality and holiness. Hence, an attack of spirituality contributed to the divestiture of my most pleasurable thing... my motorcycle. And so, I put away my toy; I sold my last bike. That was not a pleasant experience, but I felt it was a necessary one. My time had come.

The Closing of a Chapter in Life

After selling the Kawasaki 750cc Ninja to Jack Owen, the last President of the former ZMC, I bought a used Toyota Ace van and took it on several trips. It wasn't the same, of course, not nearly as much fun as riding a motorcycle. Yet, it sufficed for touring and getaways. I've lost contact with most of my old riding buddies since giving up motorcycling, with a few exceptions. This would have happened as a natural course of events anyway. It's the nature of military life and the lives of those folks involved with the military or federal government work, especially overseas. Severing friendships and frequent moves for reassignment are part of the way of life.

The years passed and my own reassignment took the family to Fort McPherson, Georgia for a final tour of duty with the U.S. Civil Service working for the Army Reserve Command. Nine months later, I retired for the second time in my life. We sold the house, moved to Southern California and settled in La Quinta. The desert offers little except what one brings to it. Our contribution was a lifetime of experience and hearts full of love. You remember the camaraderie mentioned as a benefit of membership in the ZMC? That same camaraderie ran as a common thread throughout my entire motorcycling life. It's that same camaraderie that has led me to the knowledge of where my treasure lies and to a clearer vision of the Holy Grail. At least in part, I have motorcycles, motorcyclists and a motorcycling life to thank for that knowledge and vision. These, amongst other things, have brought me to the understanding that I must first love myself in order to love my neighbor so that I may love my God. All these things lead to my inheritance: The Lord. That's where my treasure lies. That's where I will find my Holy Grail. And what about you? Do you know where your treasure lies? Are you on the way to finding your Holy Grail? I know that there is still something missing, something that ought to be there. I'm working on it. I know I'm not there yet, but that I am on the way, and hope you are too. The U.S. Army Artillery has a saying after firing a round of ammunition and waiting for it to impact on the target – "On the way, wait!"

My friends, remember this tale of a biker, and that your time will come as well. It happens to all of us sooner or later. Continue to seek your treasure and pursue the Holy Grail. In the meantime, keep on riding and hold on to those happy memories for a lifetime. Enjoy your bikes and every experience on each of them from *First to Last,* but don't forget your inheritance. You see, the end is really just a new beginning.

"Behold, I make all things new!"
(John. XXI. 5.)

Epilogue

Since retirement, the author has busied himself with composing articles about motorcycling and other subjects as a freelance writer. He still lives in La Quinta, California with his wife, Bi Yu, and he works part-time at College of the Desert Eastern Valley Campus in Indio as a computer laboratory assistant. His interest in motorcycles continues unabated, although he no longer rides. The author claims that this is not a detriment, since he often free wheels on the virtual bike in his vivid imagination. Fond memories of past motorcycling days feed his trend of thought and keep his life as a biker alive and well. He bids Godspeed to all his fellow soldiers and motorcyclists.

Lightning Source UK Ltd.
Milton Keynes UK
21 June 2010

155926UK00001B/158/A